MW00827548

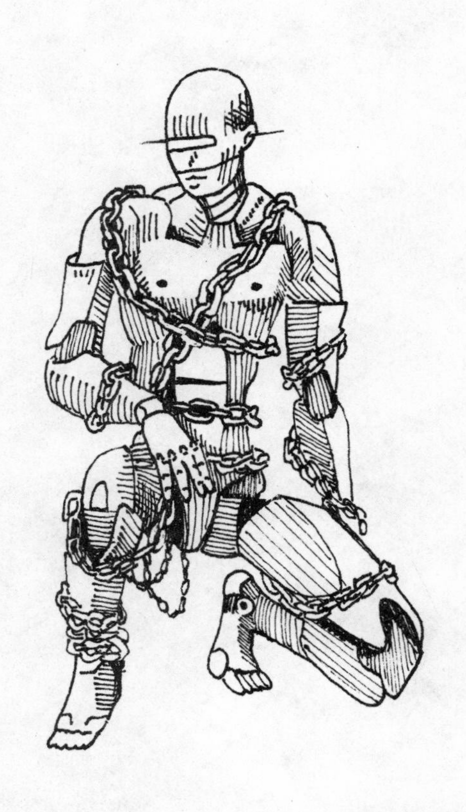

WE WANT IT ALL

Nightboat Books
New York

WE WANT IT ALL

AN ANTHOLOGY OF RADICAL TRANS POETICS

Edited by
Andrea Abi-Karam
& Kay Gabriel

Printed in the United States
Fifth Printing, 2024

ISBN: 978-1-64362-033-6

Design and typesetting by Rissa Hochberger
Text set in Neue Haas Grotesk and Lector FSL
Frontispiece illustration, "Cyborg" by Nico Gogan, 2019

Cataloging-in-publication data is available from the
Library of Congress

Nightboat Books
New York
www.nightboat.org

CONTENTS

To comrades,
lovers, friends,
dead and living.

ANDREA ABI-KARAM & KAY GABRIEL

MAKING LOVE AND PUTTING ON OBSCENE PLAYS AND POETRY OUTSIDE THE EMPTY FORMER PRISONS[1]

We're writing at a juncture of crisis—of longstanding roots and rapid progression, deeply embedded in economy and ecology and palpably felt at the level of everyday life. We're also writing in a moment of revivified theory and practice against capital and empire, characterized by widespread strikes and insurrections, an international prison abolitionist movement, the legacies of Occupy and Black Lives Matter, anti-pipeline blockades led by indigenous water and land protectors at Standing Rock and Wet'suwet'en, the rediscovery by the queer and trans left of the anti-capitalist and anti-colonial politics of the gay liberation era, revitalized labor militancy, rent strikes, housing occupations, anti-fascist mobilizations, the rapid expansion of mutual aid networks and still, exhilaratingly, more. The uprising for Black liberation that began in Minneapolis in May 2020 has further catalyzed several of these struggles, making a world without prisons or police feel suddenly like a real political possibility. Against the common-sense intuition that crisis means we must demand less, we assert with our comrades that everything has to change for anything to continue. We think of what Amiri Baraka urges in "A New Reality is Better than a New Movie!": the "scalding scenario" called "We Want It All . . . The Whole World!"[2] The title of this volume is therefore entirely literal. What we want is nothing other than a world in which everything belongs to everyone.

We have two perversions to offer to this comradely slogan. The first is the claim that, as trans people, we address this situation of crisis from a particular standpoint, or related series of standpoints, which inform how

1. Bernadette Mayer, *Utopia* (United Artists, 1984), 35: "Prison wildernesses surround most of the old abandoned prisons, they are open to the public for making love and the putting on of obscene plays and poetry readings; some are also daycare centers."
2. Amiri Baraka, *SOS* (Grove, 2013), 172-3.

we think about struggle in the broader terms of left social and political movement. The struggle for gender liberation, construed broadly as a political project instead of as a narrow fight over particular rights and recognitions, touches directly on movements for ecological and climate justice, for a world without prisons and borders, for a liberatory reworking of gender and sexual relations, and for universal access to housing and healthcare. We relate the aesthetic projects of creating alternate modes of gender and sexual life to what Kristin Ross calls the political ideal of communal luxury: the insistence that, beyond subsistence, everyone must have their share of the best. These projects of subjective liberation—of making a world for exuberant trans desire, among other modes of living—foreground bodily autonomy as an object of social and political struggle; trans people have a particular stake in a fight that, properly speaking, belongs to everyone. As a collection of writing by trans people against capital and empire, this book attempts to piece together these multiple points of overlap between the subjective, interpersonal, and everyday modes of trans life, and the internationalist horizons of the fights we are already engaged in.

The second is the sense that poetry bears on the project of imagining and making actual a totally inverted world. We don't hold that poetry is a form of, or replaces, political action. Poetry isn't revolutionary practice; poetry provides a way to inhabit revolutionary practice, to ground ourselves in our relations to ourselves and each other, to think about an unevenly miserable world and to spit in its face. We believe that poetry can do things that theory can't, that poetry leaps into what theory tends towards. We think that poetry conjoins and extends the interventions that trans people make into our lives and bodily presence in the world, which always have an aesthetic dimension. We assert that poetry should be an activity by and for everybody.

The project of the collection that follows is therefore a gamble of sorts. Can a poetics both ground itself in a particular social identity and speak expansively towards the present and its crises? Trans poetry has typically foregrounded the body, its uses and constraints, its uneven legibility, its relations to racial and colonial modes of categorization, its conscription into the wage and the working day; what else can this emphasis render into focus? How does a trans poetry translate itself across borders and languages, or account for the colonial conditions of its own emergence? What modes, beyond and together with agitprop, are capable of forcing an encounter between the ideal and the actual?

In asking these questions, we're attempting to refuse in advance the imperative of representation that the publishing industry places on trans literature. Since the so-called tipping point, opportunistic publishers have attempted to instrumentalize trans writing for profit; we're asked to transform even a brutal personal experience of abjection into titillating narratives for bourgeois readers eager to consume stories of trans pain. This process more or less represents how capital turns the precarity and violence of trans lives into cultural commodities. Tourmaline, Eric A. Stanley and Johanna Burton call representation the "trap of the visual: it offers—or more accurately, it is frequently offered to us as—the primary path through which trans people might have access to livable lives."[3] Against the trap of representation, and against the conception of trans literature as a self-interested discourse narrowly focused on securing the rights and recognitions of the state, we aim in this volume to assemble a trans poetics that both addresses and articulates itself beyond the confines of our own lives.

We didn't have to look far to encounter the overlap between trans poetry of the present and a writing that positions itself explicitly against empire and capital. This is surely in part because, as Ruth Jennison and Julian Murphet argue in their recent *Communism and Poetry*, "the resurrection of the mass action . . . has created the possibility for spatial nearness between the poet and other bodies and voices. This resuturing of poet to street has revivified the question of what poetry can do."[4] Poetry of the present, to a greater degree than a generation before, corresponds to the event of mass uprisings. On the other hand, the past decade has witnessed a groundswell of poetry by trans writers. In 2013 the editors of *Troubling the Line: Trans and Genderqueer Poetry and Poetics* could reasonably note their struggle even to find an overlap between poetry and trans communities.[5] That moment has, thankfully, passed. Trans poetry has burst the banks of any narrow canon, or even the possibility of a concise and tidy canonization. And where trans poetry in the past half-decade has exploded, it has done so overwhelmingly as a writing against capital, prisons, borders, and ecocide, animated by collective and communist desires. Our aim in the present collection is therefore both to register and to amplify this tendency—to help turn the volume all the way up on what's already going on.

At the same time, we want to link the current rise of trans radicalism to prior moments of the same, looking to the long history of queer militancy—however fraught—across social struggles and political movements.

3. Tourmaline, Eric A. Stanley and Johanna Burton, *Trap Door* (MIT, 2019), xv.

4. Jennison and Murphet, *Communism and Poetry: Writing Against Capital* (Palgrave Macmillan, 2019), 15.

5. Trace Peterson and T.C. Tolbert, *Troubling the Line: Trans and Genderqueer Poetry and Poetics* (Nightboat, 2013), 16.

By way of illustrating this intergenerational history, and thinking through the embeddedness of poetry and activism in our lives and communities, this collection includes essays from mentors, friends and revolutionaries who've passed alongside contemporary trans writing: Sylvia Rivera's "Bitch on Wheels" speech; the opening to Leslie Feinberg's *Stone Butch Blues*; excerpts from the writer Lou Sullivan; and an essay by the late Bryn Kelly on the vexed overlap of poetry and activism across generations of queer anti-capitalists. We're grateful to everyone who granted permission for these texts or put us in contact with the executors of the writers' estates. We put this work forward in conversation with that of our contemporaries, searching for a radical history for our present contexts—writing, organizing, community.

In unmaking and making a world, the poetics of this volume attempt a series of formal and linguistic experiments with political stakes. By "experiments" we mean projects that attempt a continual and creative rediscovery of their own arrangement, language, composition, and collaboration in order to stage a confrontation with a determinate moment. These experiments also disclose both senses of *radical* we mean to draw on, political and aesthetic. Whatever its shortcomings, we select "radical" as the word in English capable of evoking both idioms at once.

Meanwhile, we invoke *poetics* as a category that can combine aesthetics and politics at once, and transform the two into the formalization of a project. How can a trans poetics deploy, for instance, the techniques of collage, translation, and collaborative composition, the genres of the journal poem or the epistolary, the modes of repetition, serial composition, and direct address, the rewriting of historical or residual texts, and the declarations, excesses, and realism of the lyric? Where our sexual lives are unevenly stigmatized and criminalized, what does a pornographic writing by and for trans people look like, and what does it make possible? Where pop culture and critical theory alike have adhered to the spectacle of gender variance with a fetishizing, sadistic interest, how do trans writers creatively reply to or derange these cultural discourses? Over two decades ago, Viviane Namaste observed that "autobiography is the only discourse in which transsexuals are permitted to speak";[6] what poetic modes make it possible for us to speak in the first person while refusing or transmuting the force of that imperative to a singular autobiography? How does a trans poetics refute the singularity of so many private narratives and work towards forms of collective language?

6. Namaste, *Invisible Lives: The Erasure of Transsexual and Transgendered People* (University of Chicago, 2000), 1n3.

These questions guided our decisions in selecting and soliciting work for the anthology. We started working on this project because, in the explosion and commodification of "trans lit," we wanted to amplify writing by trans people against capital, prisons, and borders. The two of us overlap in several of our poetic desires and points of reference—like, Kay's pretty sure that she and Andrea were at the David Wojnarowicz Whitney retrospective on the same day in 2018—and we also wanted to get outside of those limits, including our own aesthetic habits and our social lives grounded in large, wealthy cities in the U.S. More than attempting to mirror our own tastes and formal strategies, we wanted to be surprised by a poem's alignment of form and political imagination. We wanted to use the volume to assemble poetic work in English from writers outside of New York and the Bay. We also wanted to move past certain trans lit clichés: coming out narratives, for instance, or testimonies to the private experience of dysphoria or social rejection. Versus the sexual moralisms of the present, we wanted to read poems that state a frank and even graphic relationship to desire—that were more interested in being exuberant and real than pristinely correct. We wanted work that articulates a keen *fuck you*, and, even in the first-person singular, invites an imagination of collective social and political stakes.

To that end, we note several patterns of overlapping strategies and concerns that emerged in the work as a whole:

(1) A tendency to braid together ecological and anti-capitalist poetics, keenly attuned to the uneven simultaneity of environmental crisis. See Raquel Salas Rivera's "soon we'll be people again" or hazel avery's "sister city."

(2) A writing-through of historical material, using juxtaposition and rewriting to think the relation of trans identity and colonial history. Cameron Awkward-Rich's "Everywhere We Look, There We Are," for instance, scatters the lexicon of Doc Trimble's arrest over the page while Rowan Powell's "(along a line a leap a landing)," rewrites the medical history of Marie Germaine (who, according to the 16th-century medical writer Ambroise Paré, leaped over a ditch and became a man) with the history of enclosures of the English countryside and the contemporary medical regulations targeted at Caster Semenya.

(3) The serial poem patterns itself on and against the repetitions of everyday life. We look for example to Harry Josephine Giles's "Abolish

the Police" series or the excerpts of serial poems from Ian Khara Ellasante, Jesi Gaston, Laurel Uziell, and Stephen Ira.

(4) The collaborative exchange licensed by the epistolary—by letters, or messages, or poems in letters. The epistolary makes it possible to speak intimately without disclosure—making it especially appealing for trans writers, who can speak about their lives without indulging a kind of prurient or sensationalizing interest in autobiography. Exchanges between Jo Barchi and Clara Zornado, xtian w. and Anaïs Duplan, and an excerpt from Evan Kleekamp's *The Cloth* enlarge a sense of the mediated intimacy and expansive thought of the trans epistolary.

(5) A palpable sense of prisons as the other side of the lyric poem's beautiful interior life. One question we're asking: how can poetry be a point of solidarity and collectivity between people inside and outside the system? We think of listen chen's line: "the social shadow explodes behind every judge's *you*."

(6) An exuberant—rather than despairing—lyricism, inflected towards pleasure, rage and embodiment in excess of or counter to journalistic description. See the contributions from, for instance, Bianca Rae Messinger, Callie Gardner, Joss Barton, Nat Raha, Rocket Caleshu, Trish Salah, Valentine Conaty, and Xandria Phillips.

(7) A turn to satire and caricature, in view of the tendency, inside and outside trans communities, to understand our lives in terms of social types—the minorly famous e-girl with 1500 twitter followers, the guy who *really* needs you to know he's a feminist, or a very nice landlord. See Amy Marvin's "The First Trans Poem," or Nora Fulton's "suqu."

(8) Intuiting a three-way relation between the abjection of trans embodiment, the grim process by which capital transforms the bodies of working people into commodities, and the enhancement and devastation of the body brought on by imperial war, several poems collected here inhabit an excess of viscera and disgust: Sam Ace, Aaron El Sabrout, Cyrée Jarelle Johnson, and Holly Raymond.

We could go on. Our intention with this partial and contingent list is to provide a non-exhaustive sense of *some* of the dynamic writing that the emergent category of trans literature has already made possible. We want everyone, everyone who wants to, to get in on it too. Every instance of these various texts and projects assembled here represents only a moment in a series of collective efforts to think about and intervene in the world we intend to win. We want it all, we want it fucking all, where *all* is a list for everyone to make.

AARON
EL SABROUT

King Krule & Mexican Street Sounds & Medicine Tea

Leaves barely shivering in the thickening stillness,
just to show that they're alive & they drink too.
The tree with the knobbly spiked flower dick
doesn't question its embodiment--it just bodies.
It is just a body. What if my body was just a body?

A motorcycle revving in the alleyway/
a masculinity built on gasoline.

Who does gender serve?
Not me, on the toilet at 4 AM
in the blue moonlight. Not a body
wracked with sweat shivers, not
the chub rub that welts slickly
between sticky thighs.

A *hudhud* cries midday, that danker morning,
calls me back to dusty Maadi lunch-as-breakfast
bisilla & *bouftek* & cucumber spears. "I was born
in seconds, do you feel me?" Somehow I cobble
this identity together in objects: this mug from
the grand canyon, this bathrobe from Winners.

But they fall apart, rotate in & out.

I too rotate in & out of bodies, out of selves,
first Pokémon t-shirt, sombrero & banana,
now notebook & paint jeans & glasses,
and then?

On the beach the wannabe Maya head
and the somewhere-maybe pyramid
are still sand, sloughing into the sea.

AEON GINSBERG

AGAINST QUEERING THE MAP

"Queering the Map is a community-generated mapping project that geo-locates queer moments, memories and histories in relation to physical space."

It feels like we're making it to easy for them this way. Watch a supremacist use joy like a blade; use a blade like a blade. Queering the map. They won't let us donate our blood but they'll let us spill it into the concrete. There's a bathroom in Taos with boot-print meant for my face. There's a customs bench on every border making ghosts of our bodies. How am I at fault for not wanting to make the one bar a gay bar? I'm content to be queer and exist; to me the impermanence of my presence is enough. The straight girl thinks it isn't gay when we kiss and I disappear into my own mouth. Ping the air quality during a smog – this is what fills my organs as I eraser myself.

The map is not clean. Operation Soap was put on by the Toronto police in the 80s: they raided gay bathhouses and arrested roughly 300 individuals. I don't fault the gays wanting to cruise and get cleansed, I fault the map. The way things are going, the queers are going to be the last haven against the police state, unless the queers give away the map to the police state. The way things are going, we will have no place to hide if the map is accessible. They won't let trans folk enlist but they're okay forcing us into prisons for trying to exist. Maybe we could make it gay for the month. Being alive that is. Or the map that holds us. Let's install closets in every corner. Maybe while we are here, it will be what we need it to be – and after, well, it could stay that way.

The government ghosts my name away from me, not even a tombstone will know how to speak it. The way it sits sounds like nothing and smog. It feels like we're making it easy to disappear our community with the internet. Upload our territories to the cloud, let it rain-hate upon us. There's nothing I can do about the gay clubs closing but let them and meet again in secret. What's the hanky code for "I want to destroy the government before I hear it say my name?" I want to be a New American Pestilence. Bio-organized death dirge. The four horses of New-Apocalypto are the Queers, the Trans, the Furry, and the Elders who lived long enough to see how to un-die again and again. It feels like the map is an excuse to have hope, in a world where we can't even afford food. It feels like we're in the maze and no one has seen cheese for decades. The queered map I want to see has a minotaur at the center. The queered map leads you into the arms of a gorgon.

A man escapes the eruption of Vesuvius in Pompei but is crushed to death by a rock anyways. That's queer history for me, always ready to throw rocks, even when we're dying; even when the world ignites our skin, says "this is how you keep warm."

BEAST GOVERNMENT

"If you are scared, I have a concrete suggestion: mask up."
—*ON SNITCHING AND THE DAYS AHEAD*

it takes those on the inside and the outside to destroy the beast. Plug me into the macro if it means a chance of destroying it. Trojan horses worked and so do Trojan viruses. Mask up. Long live the cyborg. Vaccinate the neural networks. The line between biological and technological is blurred every day. I take medication to become human, but taking the medication makes me cyborg. Bio-robotics to sustain life long enough for the Government Beast to eat us. The Geneva Convention frowns upon biological warfare and yet it's still used today. The beast walks us along the chemtrail, I'm sure if they could turn the air to mustard, they would. If we are to be the parasite, the other, the disease of the state, let us be without vaccine. If we can make the beast bleed, we can slide into its blood. If the body of the other isn't human anymore its existence biological warfare. The human body is ninety percent bacteria – we have everything we need to corrupt the beast-mainframe. The body is a microbiome, the state-body is a macrobiome. Beast-government eats the bio-cyborgs, calls it union breaking. I am almost glad to see anti-vaxxers exist for this reason alone: more diseases. Bolsanaro catches pneumonia but he should die the same way Mussolini did – upside-down in the street. All mainframes should be found in the street, heads so full of mustard you can't recognize them from hot dogs.

It could take a parasite to destroy a beast. It could take a parasite to become a snitch too. No life for a snitch is worth cultivating, but even a snitch is needed to rat out the weaknesses of the beasts of the government. Mask up. The effects of ozone death started when Euro genocide of Native Americans began, death by the millions. The beast was the first parasite, and what is there to do but become parasite for the beast. Mask up. The quality of breathable air is going down daily, mask up but literally to breathe too. There is not enough politicians alive to cause the same damage genocide has caused, and none of them are farmers either. The crops will live without the government: if the beast dies there is always produce. The further we become ourselves the further we step away from humanity. We are too full of robot-parts to return us to normal, but what makes humanity normal? Now it seems to be normal and human is to be a turkey in a rainstorm, facing the sky, mouth agape, waiting to die. It's either that or the slaughterhouse, so at least there's this choice. I'd rather get shot then pardoned by the macro-mainframe. I shoot up girl-juice to fuel up my energy against the state but, I should be just as energetic against the state as the cyborgs the state wishes to murder with me. Insulin fueled robots dying by debt. Robots unable to take trains because they lack the access to get up or down the stairs to it. The beast of the government is using pseudo-biological warfare against its biosphere. Some robots have to buy second eyes to be able to see what is happening to them. This is why the beast must be taken down before it outlives us, before the biosphere outlives it. Mask up.

It takes even the blood to drown the body. Long-kill human normal. My cyborgs have many arms to come to the beast. In those arms, many diseases.

AKASHA-MITRA

So that's what happened?!

After the great-death, the chamber dusted off its rust
like a foxdog dusting off flies.
The body that housed this chamber is subject to the natural laws.
It functioned.
It almost always did.
There were hiccups many a time, but the natural laws enslave the body.
The laws of productivity, of heartless capitalism.

This lawless chamber housed love, housed suffering, housed trauma,
and housed healing.
This anomalous chamber is made of materials both fragile and
unbreakable, unexplainable.
The vulnerable queer chamber cared for all the rust, all the lice;
All the million locked windows it sprouted every rainy day.
Now the chamber, exorcised of rust and rain, receptive to so much light,
so much air getting in through locked windows
that window panes have been banished.
The foxdog swirled in simple ecstasy—
the rust and the nails and the panes fell off.

Many months have passed since the trees moved in.
All they do now is sprout yellow flowers and entwine their branches.
Foxdogs come and sleep in the afternoons and the psychedelic-blue
velvet birds make sleazy groans all evening.

People of the *duniya* wonder what goes on inside this strange chamber :

so much impatient music, peaceful yellow halos

surrounding its rough boundaries.

The chamber now cares for the body.

The chamber has abolished walls and borders.

The chamber now—bursting with yellow flowers,

generations of foxdogs and tree folx—

has become air itself: like the blanket of air that caresses a blue planet!

It swims with the one who brought in this queer light and queer wings

which are songs.

AMY MARVIN

Hey guys

my name is Connor and I'm 59 months
on T. I have a BA in Women's Studies
and an MSW in Social Work. I landed
a tech job in the Pacific Northwest.
I'm a community organizer. I organize
socials and fundraise to organize socials.

We have a clothing swap and an office
where you can see the schedule for the
socials. We have a monthly social meeting
where you can drink craft beer. The room is
large and full of cis patrons but everyone
here is an ally. They smile at the socials.

I think of myself as an anarchist. I envision
a world without prisons or cops where
everyone has free health care and there's
enough food and beer for all to participate
in my socials. I want to see my landlord
friends and my other friends hold hands.

The Pacific Northwest and my city with
the tech job in the northwest is not perfect,
it is the best place I have ever lived.

The city is better and feels safer than any
of the other places I have lived. The city
is a great city. It is better than all other cities.

I am from the Pacific Northwest and others
are not from there. Some of these others
do not like the city despite it being the best
city I have ever lived and a better city
than all the other cities. I want to be their
friend and I hope they come to my socials.

If they do not want to be my friend
and come to my socials then they might
be mean. I do not like mean people. I
especially dislike mean girls. Once
there were some mean girls who didn't
like my social. They were not social.

I am excited to be part of the community.
There is a clinic in town that is part
of the community. It is a good clinic
for me, so it must be a good clinic
for others. This is a good community
where the people I like have good jobs.

Above all, I yearn for a world in which
everyone is vulnerable and glittery and
soft and not mean, a kinder, more docile
world full of softer signs who I can
relate to. I yearn for a world without
mean girls. I yearn for a world of socials.

This city is my city, and if it is not your
city then it must not be your city. If

it is not your social then it must not
be your social. As a community
organizer I will organize my city
with the safest, softest walls and doors.

The First Trans Poem

Every two years a trans person
who came out two years ago
declares herself an old school
transsexual. Every trans elder is

like so old now, in their thirties or
even late twenties. Every rich
trans person who just came out
is a new hope for trans people, the

one to really get this right. Every
trans person who got a media job
invented gender fluidity a year ago.
Every trans person who tracked

tenure before transing out is the leading
intellectual. Every trans person speaks
for every trans person, which is to say
there is only one trans person. Every

decade is a new trans moment, the
first trans literature, the first talk
show interview, the first trans billionaire,
the first transsexual polemic, the first arrival

of trans arrival. Every older transsexual
is problematic. Every trans discourse is
the new discourse. Every trans joke
is the new joke, told over and over.

ANDREA ABI-KARAM

TO THE COP WHO READ MY TEXT MESSAGES:

I STILL REMEMBER YR FACE. WHITE AND PINK AND SOFT W GREY HAIR. U COULD BE MY POETRY PROFESSOR, MY SUGAR DADDY IF U HELD ANOTHER SYMBOL OF POWER BETWEEN YR THICK HANDS KNUCKLES THROBBING ADRENALIN PUMPING WITH THE EXCITEMENT OF FINALLY CATCHING ME. IF U HELD A BOOK OR YR COCK INSTEAD OF A BATON CUMMING AFTER ME. I LUST AFTER THE MOMENT I CAN BECOME INVISIBLE AND PLUNGE A SCREWDRIVER INTO YR EYEBALL THE ONE ON THE LEFT THAT GLIMPSED ME FROM AROUND THE CORNER OF THE BUILDING WHOSE SHADE I SPRINTED UNDER A SCREWDRIVER WITH A FLAT HEAD TO SCRAPE AGAINST THE INSIDE OF YR SKULL WHILE YR LEFT EYE WATCHES FROM A CRACK IN THE SIDEWALK.

I HAVE TOOLS TOO.

HOLD MY HAND

in response to David W @ the Whitney DW (begun last day of the whitney DW show 9/30/18 and transcribed 11/11/18)

I

u made me want to get
fucked intensely & anonymously
hand slow, cock hard
in bright, fall/en light
break thru the
gauzy exterior of
streetlamps @ the edge of
the water @ night
the kind that eclipses
depth perception making every
thing so much more immediate
amongst the lies the institution told me
desxualizing intimacy
is a failure of visibility

II

the gradual interiority of
watching
someone flip pages & pages of
photos

of the one u/love
personal collapse slide in to icon
i wake early ready for
                    a fight
i wake early ready for
           a fuck
sometimes i think they
are just the same
gesture b/w us

the way the visual notebook
                    clicks

III

we sit
close but
& revel in this static of proximity
pressed up against DW's visual
mausoleum
people enter & exit
the grid—mid loop
we wait for the loop to repeat
anti linearity of water
falling upwards
famous gays are only
pristine when they're
dead

IV
quick cut/off

V

we sit in between gallery walls
facing others
oriented transit parallel
recordings of DW sprawl out
along the tempered light
nonstop with the weight of
mortality / immateriality / hopeless rage
i want to grab yr hand
close the blanks between bodies
in present mourning of the decades
of queer bodies propelled toward death
by state sanctioned abandonment
air bears heavy
electric net of implication in
the next phase of queer hxtory
refuse the archive / demand the
                    immediacy
of extensions pressed sharp
we breathe the same heavy air
of rage pressed play
amps crackle with loss
loosened + looping

VI

coins cascade down on to my
face + brace for
impact keep eyes open
to see where the glisten lands they recoil
on my cheeks & my eyelids & my hollows—mirrored
each shadow holding a loss @ its corners

i let the elasticity of the screen stretch over me
taut & hope i can still breathe
i wield my queerness like a leather jacket
sexy & resilient
that fine, brutal line
b/w visibility & surveillance
but god yr spiked leather motorcycle heels
are turning me
on thru the window
of incomplete desire
these zippers make me wet
i bite my lower lip & make direct
eye contact with the cycles of production
until it grinds up against me
i reveal my hardness in the space left
between red suture drawing yr
lips together blood & cum form
rivulets down yr chin caught
by my tongue along carotid
i open up in heavy prep
to get fucked by late stage cap
nonstop
for 8 hours feeling yr
hard cock @@@
then
frame—shift—click

VII

i love to watch the planes over NY
from my roof, little light grids of
transit hanging low in the sky
cmon pick me up like u did
last night @ the leather bar
the shadows of anonymity
exceed identity politics
for a few hours

VIII

"xerox former self"

IX

quick cut 2

ARI BANIAS

from The Real Me
an erasure of
Janice Raymond's
The Transsexual Empire

ACKNOWLEDGMENTS

our rage the entire

index of betrayals

our originality

our farce

our Andrea Dworkins

my lives my ethics

my early history

my world rage

its hooks

our sighs

invented destruction

found my work

my war years

with care

my telling

edits

my hasbeens

my critics rage

our cis anons

retreat

deal in hope

the diction of spirit

I spit and shit

I separate my worn id

my heads and tails

our ends divine

they wince

CONTENTS

ACKNOWLEDGMENTS

Adrienne Rich has been a very special friend and critic.

Adrienne Rich has been a very special friend and

Rich has been a very special friend and critic.

Adrienne Rich has been a very special friend

has been a very special friend and critic.

Adrienne Rich has been a very special

been a very special friend and critic.

Adrienne Rich has been a very

a very special friend and critic.

Adrienne Rich has been a

very special friend and critic.

Adrienne Rich has been

special friend and critic.

Adrienne Rich has

friend and critic.

Adrienne Rich

and critic.

Adrienne

critic.

CHAPTER II

Because realism

expanded as an illness

Because under its logics

a bird destroys

its own joy

and devotes itself

to moderation

/

Because what

enraged me

changed me

I'm divine

Withstanding

the two camps

a sweet third

Eve of no theory

CHAPTER III

Others in us

trammeled

by literalism

trust artifice

Threat

mines your

instincts

Fear can designate

Content

can shade

An entire life

stops

BAHAAR AHSAN

cut the apricot in half and remove the pit the pit can only get in your way

to live in proximity to death is to live in the space of premonition

i sit at my screen staring at an image of Abadan taken from across the water

a framed miniature sits on a shelf in my mother's home - it depicts a group of men, they are playing polo i think / or maybe performing a passion play / this image, too, is a site of premonition / me and my mother glance at it frequently as we practice new ways of relating to each other/ premonitional relationalities enabled by the hovering awareness of death

being young and naïve, i took a series of selfies at the ruins of Persepolis and released them into the stickiness of cyberspace

their afterlife is a question in which i don't hold much stake

i have removed the pit and swallowed it whole-
it is only a matter of time

a gesture
a mannerism
which signifies an affinity toward lesbian separatism

the mural was regarded as transgressive despite its having been
commissioned by the state
a remapping of martyrdom
one which is more embodied and less figurative

she swears she was both a club kid and a prophet

am i to take her word for gospel as i do when Leila Forouhar declares her love
to be a tongueless one

BIANCA RAE MESSINGER

THAT MORNING WILL FEEL QUITE LUMINOUS

for Barbara Hammer and Pauline Oliveros

everything not always visible not
possible to be so – then what will
we do tomorrow – is there any imperious
sight for us now – greying in the corner, then
that's what you did at old cafes when time was
less valuable – not against sadness exactly
or still vacant but not without character
still moving at times (keep moving they say)
not to worry then about softness returning
don't hurry it or keep our time whole on that
corner a table & a child comes up & around
barely visible then slips away – not gone
just out of the frame – then moving.
then morning morning comes & you start
licking me working down towards a now
here you are on a curb that matches the
street no disambiguation – she is
riding an elephant banging on cymbals –
giving more palliative licks – last
session – but what will we do .

FINAL NOTE REGARDING SOME ACTIONS

doing everything   at once doesn't feel like anything doesn't feel

like an action exactly a stroller passing by the window   two cops

slinking by stupidly   check the mail there's nothing there just

the story you'll tell   what it's like to

account "as much as."   – the rain comes

after many bad days my friends are mad at their lovers I love my

friends will we all be   lovers in the land of "that was it" –

one last y'know   foray –

try to flatten yourself to listen to yourself maybe a couple

friends, like one or two are better than none,

people like it – that gleaming again on the far side of the

roof, to the right, to my right. this neighborhood smells like the one I grew up in but that's 300 miles away, dear m I'm sorry I

haven't called you you must be well – well my mother says so, do I

trust her, do I trust you –

not three not flies more nasturtiums more y'know lilacs – heavy

birds "hey bird I want to be you"

BRYN KELLY

DIVING INTO THE WRECK

I met Adrienne Rich once.[1] She was speaking at a fundraiser, where I was working guest reception, and the whole thing was kind of boring for the most part. I do not remember what she said. At that time – and this was almost five years ago – she was quite frail and very much in failing health.

She reminded me of most of the women I met at the CLAGS conference on Lesbians in the 70s last year.[2] That weekend was frustrating for about a million reasons, the most palpable of which was the seeming difficulty in overcoming the intergenerational divide between the young(ish) queer academic set, and women who had lived through the 70s and were there to find community with each other, to share their work, and to remember. This lead to all kinds of unfortunate clashes, but that is a story for another time.

These women – whom my generation, for better or for worse, has (often derisively) labelled "The Second Wave" of feminism – talked a lot about their lives that weekend. The internet is a weird place. People throw up their ideas on the screen, and they are these little scratches of meaning, argument, rhetoric, and while that certainly carries a kind of power, there is another kind of power in being in a room with someone, and experiencing their words, their language embodied, their visible affects, the way they interact (or don't interact) with other people, and the amalgam of what happens as part of all that.

1. Originally posted on Bryn Kelly's blog, March 30, 2012: https://brynkelly-blog.tumblr.com/post/20162901452/diving-into-the-wreck
2. This conference, 'In Amerika They Call Us Dykes: Lesbian Lives in the 70s,' took place on October 8-10, 2010.

To break it down really simple: lesbians in the 70s had it hard, and they still have it hard. The women that I met, they were on food stamps then, and they're still on food stamps now. They were marginally employed then, trying to make art and change that no one understood, and that gets laughed at now. Their old cars break down all the time and there is never any money to get them fixed and they can't just bike around like they used to. All their spaces are gone: their bookstores, their cafes, their activist centers. They do not recognize what we call feminism as anything like the feminism they know and that has meant to so much to them; and, perhaps not surprisingly, they find our theory and our praxis highly suspect. They all have breast cancer. Some of them have had it a couple times.

Oppression creates fear, and thus, a politics of fear. I have been thinking some about that since Rich's death. There is something emotional that is catching for me: did she know, did she *really* know, how damaging her collusion on this work[3] would be to generations of low-income trans people to come? How much deep suffering and heartache it would cause? How it would bestow on us a whole new set of knives to rip each other up with?

When I see people posting reverently about Adrienne Rich in the past couple days, it inspires this panic response in me. *You are not my friend. You do not have my back. I knew it. I knew you would bail all along, and that I could never trust you, and here you are, showing your true colors. We are not on the same team. We never were. It is always a lie. Fuck you.*

I end up feeling this way kind of a lot.

My internet contacts cut a pretty wide swath through a couple different queer communities, and something like this always reminds me of how we are so different, and how difference is this gulf between people that can never be totally filled and only shakily bridged, and how all this factors into a fundamental impossibility of communication. It is a bummer.

3. At this point, Bryn's blog post included a hypertext link to a page on the website Susan's Place that is no longer active. Presumably it referred to Rich's close collaboration with Janice Raymond. See also Ari Banias's contribution to this volume.

Not to put too fine a point on it, but the people I know who are posting about Adrienne Rich break down into two camps: 1) people who love trans women and are like, "uh, hey guys..." and 2) people who do not seem to care a whole lot about us, who post uncritical gush (like I mean you would think Whitney up and died all over again). And certainly, though no one is necessarily obliged to care about trans women I guess, it all just makes me feel more isolated, more alone, more ostracized, more of a pariah, more shame, which are feelings I spend a lot of time feeling anyway.

I don't remember what Adrienne Rich said that night, but it's on the internet. However, so is a speech that Frances Goldin gave, that same night. She basically burned down the roof of the place. I will tell you, old radicals are my favorite radicals. I know it's easy to hate on newly fired-up, barely post-adolescent revolutionaries (#occupy), but it really renews your faith to meet people who have spent a lifetime busting ass and busting heads and have won a few rounds with The Man. You can really learn a thing or two from these folks sometimes.

Do yourself a favor and watch that clip all the way through! It is 8 minutes long which is like a lifetime in YouTube time, and the sound is patchy, but it's worth it. If you can't manage that, Tumblr generation, let me quote, for instance, some of her concluding remarks:

> *I wanna tell you, your life will be made sweet by comrades and friends. And it doesn't come naturally. It takes a lot of work. It takes a lot of effort. It takes chicken soup with matzoh balls when they're sick. It takes a card or a call on a birthday. It takes lending them money when they don't have it. It takes a lot of work to build friendship with the people with whom you struggle, but when you do, you get back twenty times what you invest.*
>
> *We need to get enough sleep. None of us should smoke! We have a very important job to do and we need to stay alive and be healthy, and we have to help every one of our comrades to do the same, because when we do, our lives will be made sweet, and because I do, I am truly blessed.*

Figuring out how to live together is hard. To exist in community with people who constantly piss you off is exhausting, but ultimately: worth it. As Ms. Goldin says, it is sweet. But in between, there are these things that set our teeth on edge about each other, and we start smiling the kind of smiles that are about baring teeth to each other. We don't let it show that it stings, or we shrug it off like it's no big deal, and we keep a running catalog of hurts in our head and a dossier of every aesthetic political statement everyone we know has ever made in public and index it against our own internal emotional safety actuarial matrices. And sometimes, if we trust you, we send you a text, or give you a call, or whisper to you at a party, or point blank bring it up while we're making you lunch: "Hey. Did you know you hurt me? Can we talk about that? I think I trust you enough to be vulnerable enough to tell you about this, even though it's going to make me seem like an oversensitive bitch." I suppose that's just how you get through, with other people, because the only way to get through is with other people.

CACONRAD

900 Chocolate Hearts A Minute At The Candy Factory

60

estimate number of
near-misses after
interrupting the
angel prying your
father's jaws apart
fashioned on tip of a fork
car horn at door to the birth canal
living section of dawn cooking inside the poet
today is the day we reject this vexing sell-by date worry
no guarantee we will cohere in our broken patch of garden
when you look at me you see
mostly water who will
one day hasten to
join a cloud
a thing I know for
certain is to cook
companionship into
food to taste and
become fellowship
eat a leaf with a hole
to share nourishment
with a future butterfly
you believe in sharing
at least you used to
I know you want
to shock me with
reports of enjoying
gloryholes and I can
act shocked to amuse
you yet I wonder if you
ever look up to the wall
thinking it will be his eyes

Glitter In My Wounds

first and most important
dream our missing friends forward
burn their reflections into empty chairs
we are less bound by time than the clock maker fears
this morning all I want is to follow where the stone angels point
birdsong lashing me to tears
heterosexuals need to see our suffering
the violent deaths of our friends and lovers
to know glitter on a queer is not to dazzle but to
unsettle the foundation of this murderous culture
defiant weeds smashing up through cement
you think Oscar Wilde was funny
well Darling I think he was busy
distracting straight people
so they would not kill him
if you knew how many times I
have been told *you're not like my*
gay best friend who tells me
jokes and makes me laugh
no I sure as fuck am not
I have no room in my life to
audition for your pansy mascot
you people can't kill me and
think you can kill me again
I met a tree in Amsterdam and
stood barefoot beside it for twenty
minutes then left completely restored
yet another poem not written by a poet
sometimes we need one muscle to
relax so the others follow
my friend Mandy calls after a
long shift at the strip club to say
while standing in line for death I am
fanning my hot pussy with your new book
will you sign it next week my fearless faggot sister

Encircling This Day With Centipede Coordination

Dear Eileen have we sunk the shine
the maintenance man at this place
asked if I needed help relaxing tonight
HAHA I told him to throw my door
open whenever he wanted
and HE FUCKING DID IT
when men do as I say
it saves so much time
he prolonged a certain
mediation of reality a
day when my pronoun
choice is uppity cunt
I imagine 9 things
close my eyes until
they are connected
after moving around for
years I knew if I rested to lay
his filthy hand against my chest
little critter under my tires
roadkill changing to armadillos
tell a lie to steal time for this poem
some days there is no problem
and it is terrifying
let's not get used to that
let's stop believing that
my Capricorn horns digging
pits in the Earth a surplus of
pits to bury what may
not want to let go
cars feeding crows
coyotes and vultures
he asked if poetry
could possibly fulfill me
but it is the study of everything

Impaled By Sharp Points Of Wonderment

he
insisted
I should know
names of extinct species
as though taxonomy ever meant preservation
telling someone who they are
instead of asking is where
extinction gets its start
another window into the
carefully ornamented shadow
you call tails while the
double-headed coin
flies through the air
you say the new
prison means
good paying jobs
for generations
this is where I expect my vomit to land
you start using your therapist as
a weapon against your friends
you pay to be told new
furniture cannot combat
the death of your bedroom
I imagine prison guards not yet born
having lunch inside their parents
study design of the owl's
feathers to study
arms race of
the night

You Cannot Return A Stretched Mind

68

human life expectancy is rising
I ask which group they mean
no one knows the answer
my favorite lovers were
men who knew they were dying
they taught me to race to my limits without hesitation
sometimes it takes more death than I can endure to caress life
if you could have seen my face the moment I realized no help was coming
despite every dream of
lovers around the
globe uniting
grateful for our embrace to
hold the sadness different
we are too fragile for the
world we are making
pretending to be tough
a sudden fear of heights over the Atlantic
flock of dead lovers leaving with the geese
transmit psychic code to *go Go GO*
saying AIDS aloud enters
each body uniquely
cells memorize
all abyss survived
please say today
is the day we
accept our
family
as every
neighbor

CAELAN ERNEST

four perspectives (of the same object)

perspective 1:

an old lover in the latex bunny costume. the room
surrounding their body appears to stretch
with no sense of end. from this perspective
the subject looks to be encased. the old lover
performs a dance that's not so much a dance as it is ritual
or a ceremony commencing the hunt. i'm nowhere
to be found.

perspective 2:

the orgy is an archipelago. the bodies appear to move
in & out like Pangaea, forming & unfurling until
all that skin obscures the optics around adjectives such as 'disobedient'
& 'unruly.' the mass, having come together,
shakes the room in its feral mosh pit— the many
tremors it leaves in its wake.

perspective 3:

my body. strung up across the walls
of what appears to be a museum. beneath it,
a television set draped with ratty headphones

& a bowl of rock candy. members & visitors
of the institution alike listen to the sounds
my voice makes in the video in the earphones like a brass
instrument synthesized / digitized for semi-mass consumption.

a child, bored, reaches for a piece of candy
until what's presumed to be her mother tells her
to spit it out. a man extends his arm to grab me
but the sound of a siren wails throughout the room
causing everyone to rush out before he can make contact.
as they go
i hear a voice say the exhibit would've been more profound
if the artist hadn't put me in that disheveled blonde wig.

perspective 4:

a bird. a swallow, maybe.

CALLIE GARDNER

LOVE & RAGE, & RAGE

1.

waiting unbecalmed, i assist in
tempestuous attentiveness;
i work at the mailbox,
& see how are we here for
the manipulation, the impression
made with certain (forbidden) sharps.

i open the hatch,
look down;
something shouts back
your worst contributions.

it moves slowly
yet unpredictably,
with painful skin.
would i sew scarless hands on—
i especially miss them today,
in this tshirt weather of midwinter spring;

& the data that has built
up beneath us
is subtle & perilous,

surrounds sound more like
a sweet loss,
& those it does not
break it just kills utterly,
& i thinkalot like:
what if that were me;

i need a new location,
acquaintance;
i will no longer be answering emails
at this address, &
i need new words for all my feelings
because they
(i need a new pronoun for this)
were misused;
i need to be able to speak of
your prominence, &
i need, when you are knighted, to be able
to ride off into the forest,
i need nobody & everybody to know
what (who) you really are (like)

2.

my friend says that you
are one of the only people
she would punch in the face.
i don't want to punch you in the face.
i don't want to punch anyone in the face.
i know i should—
fascists & terfs—
that i should find a red gym in my area,
get strong for the bashing back—
but i don't.

i want *(instead?)*
to learn to punch faces
in a gentle but devastating way,
like modernity,
or a lifestyle blog,
or non-recyclable plastic;

i want to make the enemy so
anxious they crumple in the street, so
depressed they can't leave their beds;
does the impulse then remain good & pure?

3.

send needs
through breakthrough speech,
seeking arrangements
that involve me being found
in the clearing of violets,
& for the extreme motion
against energetic sensations of new
personhood.

love too be an incantation, with
infractions' reversal upon terror sides—
as bodies plotz fireworks of coins
i feel like ramona flowers,
constant comment & aries moon

(& you, whom all my poetics have evaded
who gave me shit & took none in return:
in the movie james spader will play you);
whereas living motionless in the old world,
wearing on like how we do,

i pacify myself with sugar & guts,

if i work back to the present without delay,
we will get grievous & gross with it,
tongues heavy & salty & here to stay.

CAM AWKWARD-RICH

Everywhere We Look, There We Are

A MALE IMPERSONATOR.

Dora Trimble, a black female, who has been masquerading around as a man under the alias of "Doc Edward," yesterday had to pay dearly for her masculine propensity. Dora did not like the frills and ruffles of femininity and the hundred other appendages of womankind that made her a prisoner of custom, so donning a pair of jeans, brogans, an elongated cap and other apparel usually worn by the sons of Adam, she paraded herself about as a man and a bully. She miscalculated the limit of her self-named privileges, and wandered into the domain of the bluecoat. So to speak, she was thereupon disrobed of her cunning character and turned over to Second Recorder Marmouget for disposition. The Recorder got rid of his charge in a few minutes. It was $10 or 20 days for Dora, and in default of payment of fine, she was given nine days additional board and lodging at the Parish Prison.

[In the next room, wailing. Man woman other can't tell. Any human specificity obliterated by pain. Someone walks into the room where I am pinned. Looks at me, my paperwork. Backs away shaking his head]

Doc

it

has been

yesterday

for

a hundred

hundred

days

yesterday

elongated

into

a Prison.

to

day

a black female,

disrobed of

her

son

black

dear

got rid of

by

black

appendages

of the bluecoat.

bully *bluecoat.*

self-named privileges

Doc

days

turn over

It
has been *yesterday*

i

wander
the blue

minutes

disrobed

[As child, I too was an
impersonator. I had a
body &, also, a life that
moved with no regard
for form.

God willing, my will
carry me]

o *im*

fine,

i *m*

fine

[that long honeyed pause between *I am* and *caught.*]

dear

prisoner

dear

alias

appendage

elongated

limit

parade

of

black

black

cunning

black

$

black

frill and ruffle

dear

Doc

dear

other

i

dear

woman

man

self-named

CASPAR HEINEMANN

Ferocious Lack Harmony

when we picture the end of the world i hope
we can find it adorned with rose blossom and
a million bonfires of dead cops as literal as you like
a fountain spilling the cracks in the foundation
alluding to an absence of base of superstructure you
know the thing i mean i hope when we picture the
end of the world is an opulent credits sequence without
names my primary metaphor for the death of ego is
dumpling stew we can all be dumplings darling it will
be warm and undistinguished a haphazard orgy of
slightly better weather than we currently experience
simply through our altered perceptions of better a
magnificent collapsible spittle diamond against progress the
new cum will taste so good as good even as the old
cum our rapidly expanding human animal consciousness
ricocheting of the walls of the space time continuum
an infinite percentage of that also containing the
redundancy of digital marketing executives it is
going to be so beautiful i hope when we picture the
end of the world fire feels hotter yeah we want it all fucking
gross and fucking twee up against the wall motherfucker
remember men me neither i might have even been one imagine
the end of the world the abolition of egg white omelettes
nothing less than fully bucolic bourgeois hobbit utopia

tropical islands gay ramblers association of the mind
at a leisurely breast stroke pace i'm regressing again
but all i hope is when we picture the end of the world
we end the picture of the world

CHARLES THEONIA

THE PEOPLE'S BEACH

on your leash I'm accounted for
femmes cuddle up on the sand
you grab my ass   say you like
to see us enjoying each other
driveby stench of the water
pollution plant   police copters
agitate overhead   they dragged
a guy naked down the boardwalk
when his towel fell   up beach
private hammocks   palm trees
for rent   vs. nutcrackers
on our seedier
stretch   rosy lizard
insides   sticky lychee
skin   I'm reading
Bob Glück's gyroscopic
nipples   you're pursestrung
under pasties   honey gauze
dissolving stitches   me I'm years
out   and still livid pink
    resolution?   I don't know her
we sink in   even the book is sweaty

THE COLOR OF JOY IS PINK

the pink of us is inside and highly specific
community goes on nebulizing outward forever
wouldn't you rather pick an affinity group
or three we'd get into more and better trouble
that way than in the Brooklyn Volunteer
Accountability Corps where the creeps
just walk off regardless into the forever of us
but the more of you is better and every day
you never read the books I like
even when I buy them for you twice
and still the color of us is I bet you
wouldn't unless you knew I was looking

all along the self keeps atomizing and joy
is a shared term I don't know the name for
I'm here for rent parties or to hold your hand
in the hospital where the self of us is more
contested than ever and other unnecessary
untruths when you have everything right here

everything's not enough I know it never is
enough is the color of you me and the rest of it
let's cut your hair plus drink each day a little

less and recommit to slipping further as it
happens I'm not doing anything but this

with Diana Ross

CHING-IN CHEN

Behind the Ballroom

because we agreed no octopus in light
gross butches laugh multi-color drop green skin at midnight wait
because we twenty-three mushroom clouds fuzzy white sun to die
all blue hair here all
orange electrical systems aflame all violet storms at our fingertips
I drove you home to cardshack hoped
a spiked little girl best pastel would rinse me
tidings
I don't want to skim our song dead all perfectly
cold chalk lines
street blue star take all orange victims we count up green stalk
tilt who lost
40 37 29 66 lucky numbers
who still remember ranks when we swell to black
fighter in aluminum squad we marooned each other still filled
four walls heavy and sedated disappear and re-align grassy ditch

watching couches loving empty house
our marching orders shapely and efficient our dearly departed
costs
welcome to neighborhood drum bbq and makeshift boombox church
I leave daily for that highway life

born a string of golden light I invited my growing mother

Household Mutations

after Carmen Agote

to new baroque bedroom   she said who wants radioactive suitcase
who invites one lined with silver teeth
who mirror white   wants whale carpet scraped from mattress of maps

all routes poured with last tea   *all routes spilled from me*, all her nights
attached to appliance   dainty shoes unwrap ears

those stains belong to me, all her shoulder-leaning   crease my joints
all snaps in cups shave head to a cut   all bikes and doorways remember
I came to alter   to table without
a fight

Returning to a Posted Notice Taped to the Door

because the spiked-eye girl grew up

to man the black and white office
hello in fading light

growing daily with mud

threaten smiley face come to sell
you your house back before Emancipation
Park opens.

camera, you're on poem blast.

a lemon surface reflecting hands
I leave daily for that highway life
though green doorway don't nod heads or say
There's a feathered lawn
each morning calling for honey

we just input
a red field of tongues
in the visitor's log a

Joke on you – we're renters.
Joke on you – smiley face

Trying to Feel Human/Tomorrow

I never saw a fast-drying pigment never saw those
seven black hills again *build an eye cheap*

behind redacted siren walls those stitched rivers drifting in a book
really a grid builds an eye for a workhorse cheap I never saw redacted sirens

never saw the network translate dusty harm
wall the network
counting smooth those flights up highway
each unit count smooth
seven lanes return
to a sea of cement walking seven lanes

what returns *Never Came*

a final word across the sea

Self-Portrait, house with no one present

in expectant house milk
memory alone on porch we
all borne from fat
chemical

to sleep and take up
all moist names on off-
color stone mixed
a generation
on branch of that milk-
raised hunger

country
allowed maps of fire claims two generations
uncle visits in grass spreading
pegs of his own celebration and pretended
to be cousins
a succession of hands visits shopping per usual for parts
heard no trash calling
me back home

all smoothed away then we all write our names in stone

CLARA ZORNADO AND JO BARCHI

Correspondence on Erotics and Karaoke Rooms

Jo,

When I first moved into my apartment, I excitedly taped a notecard with mine and my roommates' last names written in all caps onto the front of our mailbox. Two years ago. The sun has since bleached away any and all signifying information, so it's unlabelled, and I am liable to receive or not receive any and all mail. I keep forgetting, because it seems like I still get all the right mail. But I guess I wouldn't know. This is all to say, Xxx's wedding invitation came in the mail this week. As it stands now, I'm driving to the wedding, to Chicago, in October. I'll see her get married, I'll see you. The fantasy is that every project I'm working on now will be done by then. The fantasy is that the rest of my life exists in October, and nothing can preclude it. We'll get to reflect on how the summer was tough but brilliant, how the year ahead looks even more fruitful. I am so ready to enter the world that has my completed projects in it.

I've had a Susan Sontag interview taped to my bathroom wall for over a year and I took it down this week. Watching everyone laud themselves on having read Notes on Camp got to me. I haven't read it. And I don't want to jump into talking about Lady Gaga but I did watch all sixteen minutes of her Met Gala entrance and thought it was exquisite. She shares her excellence so well. Tried to read a book today and I couldn't even take in the preface. Then I took a break. Now I'm writing you. I struggled with some of the articles you sent me, are letters just a way of taunting their recipient? I don't agree. I think a very active part of my ethics is not taunting people, so I don't see letter-writing in that way - there's that implicit sense of patience even in my most explicit letters. Thinking of a past email to my friend Xxxx: referencing him giving me head and then immediately inviting him to linger before writing me back. Like, *please take your time getting back to me*, but also, *feel free to give me some time*. It wasn't hot so much as personal. And I could've been so coy, right?... So, what's erotic in the epistolary? I think passivity in all communication is a turn-off, and that the least taunting, most intimate thing to do is to ask for something because you'd love to have it. Read my letter and see if you *want* to write back. That's an invitation. For you.

I keep thinking about how [X] recently cut me in half, we were talking about how I always post about emotional work on Instagram. They said, "I always think to myself how hard it must be to be you, Clara." I turned away because I started to cry. And we were at [X], so then I had to laugh it off: "I don't know how else to be!" I hate betraying my own boundaries like this. Faltering instead of explaining, "I don't feel like I'm growing if I'm not uncomfortable." All this is to say, I spent a lot of time today considering the ways in which I can be an enemy to myself. Phrasing them as powers. Knowing which are acts of resistance and which are harmful: my flexibility and compassion can often lead to a lack of discipline; I've spent so much time learning to set boundaries that I often fail to enforce them. I appreciate, in AA, the crucial task of considering the vast landscape of one's character assets and defects. I am trying to relish in the diligence of all my practices, because I don't know how else to be. I've loved our recent conversations about prayer because that's all I want to talk about. The opportunities for serenity that exist in resentment, and how prayer grants us access to them. That's all I want to talk about. In my dreams, there's a miniature karaoke bar and we are both there, sober. It's pure.

When I took down the Sontag interview, I replaced it with "Italo Calvino: In Memoriam." The first line goes, "the death of a writer is like the death of the sun." What could it be like to be loved like this. There's severity there. What kinds of softness could be in the sun, though...? Thinking about all the things I'll never have memories of. Getting sad. Thinking about reading poems at funerals. Not sure why I put this obituary on the bathroom wall. Feeling like this question is extremely dehydrating even though no one's making me answer it. Oh: here I am, taunting myself, maybe.

Last notes: you said your aura is orange and I said it feels like you. Orange is a color I don't know very well but it does really suit you. Sweet and brazen. Safety color. Googling how many aura photographers there might be in Chicago. October. RevealingSoul.com says it can reveal the energy of my soul. Let's go?

P.S. Whatever song you think would be playing at the miniature karaoke bar in my dreams, is playing.

Talk to you soon,

Clara

Clara,

When I first moved to Chicago, taping up a name card was all I dreamed about. Having an apartment. Having a place with my name on it. I've never taped up a name card. I've always been too lazy, too forgetful. It's never materialized. My name still isn't next to my roommates. It's been almost 2 years in this apartment. I wonder if I'm getting all the mail I'm supposed to. I must be. I don't really feel that I'm supposed to be getting any mail. All my bills are paperless. All my bills are paid late.

When I think of anyone I love visiting Chicago, it's always in August. This has been a running theme for years. People I love always crowd the city in that month. It's already too emotionally full for me. It's the month of my sobriety date. It's the month I first moved to Chicago. It's the month where summer feels endless and I feel useless. All I mean to say is that I'm happy you won't be here in August. The malaise always wears off by October. We can sit and talk and talk. Have I ever told you that whenever I first see you after a long period of separation, I don't know what to say. I never know how to start the conversation. And then suddenly I feel like I can't say enough, I can't listen enough. I love this about you. I love this about us. I can't wait to sit and try to figure out where to begin. There will always be something I forget to mention.

I have so many projects I want to share with you. I have even more projects I want to make with you. I still hope we spend a summer week writing an album together someday. Every project I'm working on lately ends with an object. A book. A film. Something I can physically hold. I'm trying to grow out of that. I wonder if I will have by October.

I'm also in the group of people who haven't read notes on camp. I've read virtually no Sontag. I own Illness as Metaphor. I stole it from the brown university bookstore back when I still lived in Rhode Island. I own her journals. That's what I'm most interested in. I know at some point she says male homosexuality is narcissism. I think she's right in a way that I can't defend, which is to say, I feel it. It rings true and makes me want to scream.

I haven't watched the full video of Gaga at The Met Gala. I believe it's magnificent. Her outfits were amazing. I wonder what we would wear if we were invited. I imagine we would go separate years. I believe our trajectories are different. I have a feeling you would be there before me. I would celebrate this if I'm right. The themes will be different then. I have no way of predicting what we would wear, but I imagine we'd both wear yellow.

I'm writing back to you now, later than I said I would. I am always late in writing back, and sometimes I am early in writing first. I don't know if I read the articles I sent you as saying that the letter is a way to taunt. What I remember being struck by is the idea that the letter is a way to talk about oneself. Is that a taunt? It can be. I sometimes enjoy talking about myself in a way that taunts someone into talking about themselves. then again, I think I don't taunt often, I mostly invite. for better or worse. I love that you invite too. A lack of the explicit is the biggest turn off for me. Say what you mean. Throw it out there and let it fall on me. That's my greatest fantasy. Someone telling me the truth.

You bring up the concept of erotics. I love this. I find erotics so enticing and hot, mainly because I don't know how to define it. I don't really know what it means when people use it, but I know how it feels. I know when something is erotic because it connects with my chest. It's anything from smut to a letter. A letter to me is erotic because I don't always know what it means, but I want to. The epistolary is erotic because the truth is told, or is hidden. I don't claim to know what everything means, but I do claim to be turned on when I learn.

The idea of lingering before writing back speaks to me. I'm always running late, but maybe that's just because I'm in a constant state of grieving, of having to let it linger. I once again don't claim to have all the answers.

Being emotional on the internet, being intentional and open about the growth we want isn't for everyone. It can be corny when done wrong. It can be read as antagonistic to those who aren't doing the same work, who wish to avoid doing that work. My sobriety has been taken as antagonistic more times than I can count. People begin defending themselves after I mention that I quit. People find an indictment in anything. I understand this. I am defensive. I am always reaching for a reason to dispel any criticism. I am blaming so often. As I write this I realize I am telling an old story about myself. This isn't true anymore. It's where my mind goes at the first moment of criticism, but it never lasts. It passes. I accept the responsibility.

Having a job to me feels like a betrayal of my boundaries every day, but that's just to say that I don't feel built for it. I don't feel built for caring about my labor. I feel built for caring about myself and my loved ones. I feel built for saying fuck your coworker, and fuck any boss I've ever had who has told me I'm not doing a good enough job. I don't care.

I feel like I'm responding to myself and I want to return to what you've said. I am not growing when I'm comfortable either. I am betraying myself semi regularly, even with the continued growth I am engaging in. I engage in lacks of discipline even as I grow up and become closer to the most helpful and realized version of myself. This is fine. I am not an enemy of myself. The step work you bring up, from AA has been crucial in this. Acknowledging and knowing where my defects lie. Understanding where those come from. It's all survival to me. I can forgive myself surviving. I can forgive myself almost anything. If I can't, I would be dead. that 's dramatic. It wouldn't be death. Just deep spiritual misery.

Prayer grants us access to everything, even if it's slow and not what we want access too. It's not the knowledge I crave, not the library style mind I wish I had. It's the knowledge that somewhere there does exist serenity. Somewhere in me. When I let go. When I believe in that karaoke room that we aren't in, but could one day be in. When we are there it is pure, and when we aren't it continues to be pure. We can sing whatever we want to each other. No taunting. Like siblings sharing a bed, a little stoned. Singing along to a warped record. Falling asleep.

Taunting yourself, sadness, poems at funerals, obituaries. All of this feels like a necessary part of creating to me. Or rather, to be less and more cliche, this is a part of the lives we have built for ourselves. Most days I love my life. When I don't work too hard. When I sit with a book. When I pray. When I actually write. When I write to you.

My aura is a deep orange. There is yellow in there. I realize as I type this that the colors in my hair and the colors in my aura aren't very different. I am sweet and brazen. This is something many could say about me and sound insightful. When you say it I know what you see and I know what you mean. When we laugh.

Lately I've been thinking of that time we were walking up the stairs to get to my mom's apartment. After some show. It was late. I said we had to be quiet. You said *I'll be quiet* in the voice of a wounded child. We both broke down hysterically. The walls of that hallway weren't exactly orange, but when the sun shone right. They could be.

I don't want to say what song I dream about playing in our karaoke room. I want to keep it secret. I don't want to have to choose one. We both switch it up so well. We could do a three hour residency there and still miss songs. In October we'll do it all. Karaoke. Aura photos. The whole thing.

I love these soundtracks of ours. I love this laughter of ours. I said recently that I wished I had written a love letter. You reminded me that I could've, that I could've written you back. We both laughed. I hope you know this is my best attempt. I do love you.

Text me,
Jo

CODY-ROSE CLEVIDENCE

POLLINATE; BY HAND

POLINATE .by hand /dysph
or [aria{ "of th state of th flesh" what
is this [my nest] go down,
Calliope, catastrophe, my eros
from whim 2 prayer [each
wing bare | o sun o this
weird communion—]
{} several aphorisms: "th throats
of stallions th throats
of egrets th throats
of men." – 2 get a grip
on [[oneself, like that—
[show me] own hive
aswarm in sunlight, own hive,
my hand, palm up [o sting]
so soft what's this
new thing in me | in this
dizzying carousel of
dew n dawn n sunday
afternoon () which kind
of coward are you, which
am I—

Untitled

OF TH UGLIEST FLOWERS I say this it's a shit world my petunia stuck
in an obscene gesture of delight. you get to keep what is inside of you, in some
sense, if you can hold it here before it changes into something else, though at
some point we all have to reconcile with the real; th angels | at their nest—
polyhedrons that do or do not exist— being an organism with needs & desires
& th capacity for excruciating pain. I call th flowers ugly but it is something in
my heart— "this, after all, is why we do most of what we do, to control what our
senses will encounter." — 2 become particulate: 2 go from "shuttup bird" to "shut
up yellow-throated warbler" – take me home night hawk in th high hard dusk
particulate. in th lilac of my eyes. where I have placed a cold hard stone. how 2
transcend all th things is a question of th real. how 2 hold th ringing inside you a
question of springtime. how to impel th sensory organism of yr body toward an
imagined joy is a question that hovers between biochemistry & th void. jk. it is a
question of desire, and nailing a certain trajectory. is it th need of th bark that calls
up th sap. do the blades of grass quivering in chilled darkness elicit dew. I think th
world evolved organisms to feel it. to crawl across its surface impelled or repelled
by th feeling of it. to hold it inside of them. which we do.

NOTHING MAKES SENSE ABOUT THIS FLOWER

"because it would mean they have forgiven us"
—George Oppen

desire's steep rush, pasture
of atonement, cherries grown from seed—
"the kingdom of heaven" is not so great. The Dawn
is not so great. Behind th dawn there is another, bigger dawn.
When I have gone rapturous, before th fold,
when I have gone and gotten myself
fucked w th world, th worded-ness of th world,
leaf-green, pheremonal, probably drunk, crawling with
such sensations, when I have gone and tended
what wants tending, hellebore, hollyhock, angel of mercy,
don't flinch. When gods hold each other down— with
a gentle yet terrible force— yes, o make of this
th waterfall, th "glory" of th "godhead"—
thy rod and thy staff, just kidding, they
comfort me, We are already late for th threshing
"for th harvest of earth is ripe"— I do not know
how still th waters will be, where we are going, or
how green th pastures, it is already already summer, kneel down.
There is wretchedness upon th earth and many goldfinches
there is something caught in th air, here, where we are becoming
reciprocal animals, look— I hold in my hand two
cherries, and don't know how to ask
permission.

"FOR THOSE ABT TO ROCK, WE SALUTE YOU"

th great rope which tethers earth 2 sky, bound
at th wrists and ankles, gently
but with a terrible force, Andromeda, my breath—
th condensation on th glass—reach up—
o each body, weird body— arms, legs, feet—
extant in space—
to ask | 2 b christened
by all that gathers in th cool dusk—
--to stand up— what is it that gathers
in th cool dusk
at yr face— yr hands, unbound,
open now, to let th cool air though, whole
night, each season, no rhyme, no nothing,
pitched forward, where yr lips have passed over in silence
th stillness of yr autumn th shallow waters
of th lake of yr heart full of frogs,
eels and fish and small molluscs, small rocks,
a yellow-crowned night heron stalking them
on th white riverbed, th berries
are done, th geese are going, th lake
is driven dark and mad w wind, th bluedark sky
of yr heart, when it has stopped raining
and I am in th meadow still, untethered from th sky
and all around is wind, wind, th clouds

driven across th sky in all directions
and the geese are flying south again
and every word you speak is false
and th sky like an idiot runs itself into th ground, drunk,
staggering—scattering th small hard seeds
[[are those horns— where is th moon— I don't
know— how to help you— now—]]
before wheeling off again, seeking
its leash, its
palm & open
pasture wider,
farther on.

CYRÉE JARELLE JOHNSON

harold mouthfucks THE DEVIL

Harold is 52. He drives roundabout 66 miles on I-95 to and from the tube factory
in Branchburg. He punched the glass over the speedometer yesterday. The automobile's

tools of measurement are bloody, but he never checks them anyway. The cupholder
clutches a 3/4s empty can of Budweiser. It's 6:15 in December and the moon is maroon

in the black latex of Pine Barren sky. His backseat is tetris'd with cans of O'Doules.
Nice try, Harold. A white streak darts through the road as if chased. Harold's nausea

pulls the string beneath his tongue, presses its thumbs into his throat. He opens the car
door a little, its leatherette split from heat. It's as though his insides are tearing
as puke punches through him, bilious, no longer containing food or even beer.

He lays on his back in the puddle he made, only an inch too shallow to drown in.
A figure above him. Behold, a goat; its ocular golden cleft. Harold's bleary eyes peer

and correct. The goat stands dripping stygmata and flexing bicep tattoos.
Solve. Coagula. The goat has titties and a dude's face and no genitals to speak of.

The thing no one ever told Harold about THE DEVIL is that when you see them
you get uncontrollably aroused. Sexually. Harold doesn't like any gay shit

he ran off his eldest stepchild at 14, who is me, the narrator. Kicked his face and ribs
until he fled and in her fear the mother called it justice. But here he is, cock stiff before

THE DEVIL

THE DEVIL strides closer to Harold on cloven hooves, in leather assless chaps,
unbothered
because they're THE DEVIL. Although THE DEVIL doesn't have a binary gender
expression

it's still gay to Harold. THE DEVIL values consent so they ask Harold
if he would like a fellatio and Harold nods and screams *YES! YES!* 6 covens
of genderless magical practitioners arrive for orgies nearby because THE DEVIL
is into that. Everyone in the vicinity is on the verge of ecstasy when Harold starts to cry.

THE DEVIL turns the burnt out O'Doules cans into piles of glistering gold coins,
and we stimulate
ourselves with their ridged edges. Harold snatches his boxcutter from the pocket of
his vacant jeans.

He slits his own throat. He's dead and he's gay and he's not sure which is worse.

EVAN KLEEKAMP

from The Cloth

The plants died even though I watered them. My apartment was in shambles. Books, for example, lay in piles wherever I had slept. Receipts and paper scraps on which I had written aphorisms, on which I had written things I told myself to do but had never done, on which I had written about exhibitions that in some cases I had attended, as well as quotation after quotation without attribution (there were several of these), the occasional email address or phone number (these rarely made their way into my smartphone), but especially those on which I had written the names of painters such as Agnes, Eric, Jutta, Krebber, Laura, Monique, Quaytman, Ruth, and Stevie. Frequently, I tucked the scraps between the pages of my journal, where, seemingly preserved, they kept their asymmetrical folds. What did you not want me to see? read a discarded note I later found underneath the sofa. Another receipt listed terms: Epicenter, Node, Contract, Module, Snapshot, AutoBio, Episode, Moebius Strip.

I began writing a novel. My novel will be about a person who carries a flower between their legs, I decided. As if a flower could infect someone. I became concerned with the methods for entry. Had I provided enough points of view? Was the writing clear? I thought of you of all people. I wanted to give you access, to give you passage into me.

During all this mental commotion the flower grew. It grew until it fell over, then it wove around my leg. I kept a journal in which I wrote the date in the style of European newspapers at the top of the page. Hours passed imperceptibly. I couldn't keep track of time because the days and hours repeated. I conflated myself with others who surrounded me. I hardly knew who they were. Case in point, the figure in the mirror regarded me in a way that I could not regard myself. Negotiating with the figure, I asked, Was there a way to go? An interface I might toggle? A method that would allow me to systematically advance? Was this how things were going to be?

I had no means or reason. I found a note written on a bookmark at the bottom of my purse that said: *Gathered Evidence*. I had a purse. Wasn't that astonishing? I was getting dressed in the mirror, rummaging through my bag. Only evidence, I thought. Occasionally drawings, other times writerly ephemera. I imagined a book that could function as a place of rest. Like a room in which you slept and woke simultaneously.

But what was happening? Didn't I want to remain unseen? My reflection, was it truly mine? Sometimes it felt that way. My earring shone in the mirror as if possessed by someone else. Like the flower between my legs, the mirror inside my heart, too, resided virtually within the surface where I examined myself. I slept on a sofa Kim had left me that pulled into a bed. I slept in the living room, beside the front door. Sometimes I slept with the door and the windows wide open to admit a cooling breeze. In addition to the sofa, Kim had left me a dress with pink and green flowers repeating across its black fabric. She had given me the dress after I tried it on.

I had no idea what the dress was, what it was doing. But, like the flower, it was occurring inside me. Lesions broke out across my back and in the crevices of my arms. I took mineral baths to moisturize my skin each night before resuming sleep. Before resuming what I thought was sleep, which at times felt like staring straight up at the ceiling light even when my eyes confirmed the room was dark. My nonexistent husband rubbed oils and creams on the region I couldn't reach between my shoulders. One time I stopped him so I could add another card to the wall. I would write entries from my journal on notecards and then pin them to the wall in the living room where Kim had kept her television. I pinned them to the wall in a grid. This, after spending months sleeping in the living room because I didn't have a proper bed. The grid fanned into an enigmatic cross that branched along its vertical axis: a hopscotch pattern resembling a question mark. Face, Mask, Shield, Bodyguard, Signal, Decoy, Target, Sign, Mime, Museum, Aberration, Anomaly, Repression, Detour, Omen, Totem, Ambiguity, Context, Ruse, the cards forming the grid read. As an experiment, I approached the wall, closed my eyes, and removed a card at random. I did my best not to look. I folded it twice into a square and then tore it along its folded edges, which left a diamond-shaped hole where the words had been. When I returned the card to its spot on the wall near the center of the grid, the other cards seemed to nod along and concur. But upon closer inspection none were missing.

I took a picture.

I was naked in the first image, and then wore the dress in the second. In both photographs, my body appeared on the right side of the tableau, inside the mirror. A pillowcase covered the lamp behind me. A gray cloth suspended by a golden rail, I thought. A damp flag pierced by golden beams. I remembered John Berger describing Francis Bacon's 1970 *Triptych, Studies of the Human Body* in which, according to Berger, a woman crawls along a rail. Like a child, he emphasizes. How could an image be a woman? Crawling like a child, did Berger mean the woman crawled with uncertainty? Without knowing the next step? Without necessarily knowing if she would be able to continue? Was Berger suggesting the woman was unconscious as to what propelled her? Unconscious about the rail along which she crawled?

Each day was like this. Forgetting what I had read or seen as means of remembering it. Questions for which I could furnish no answer, questions that seemed to elliptically posit themselves. Was I a man wearing a dress? A dress exterior to a woman? At the time, I was considering my relationship to erasure. In fact, I was beginning to understand my ability to blot out the past. I liked that phrase. Blot out the past. It made me think of an eyedropper that sucked up then disseminated clear liquid across the white sheet twisting in my head. Upon reflection, my childhood suggested an ability to delete myself with ease. I thought about the number of experiences I simply couldn't remember. I thought about running away from home as a child. Knowing that I had done it but relying on minute glimpses from the past to patch together what may or may not have taken place.

Then you crossed my mind.

I saved the images I took of myself beside the notecards and sent them to you. I couldn't forgive myself. Forgive myself for what, I didn't know. I had looked in the mirror, seen my ribcage and my hips, then you came to mind. That's what I remembered. But my nonexistent husband loved me. How could I want more? You wouldn't go away. I found another card that said: I'm not asking for punitive measures or forgiveness, I won't let you misunderstand me. That much seemed true. The flower tightened around my leg. Desires coiled around me as if they were my own. The cats outside cried to be fed. They cried to me as if I were their mother. That night, at the end of my dream, I stood in the bathroom. I decided I would shoot myself. I turned the faucet to the right, in the direction it usually does not go, and then entered the shower. Through the window, I could hear a helicopter fly overhead while warm water pooled underneath my feet, began to travel upward along my leg.

It was early in the morning when I woke on the sofa. My nonexistent husband had left the front door unlocked. I smoked a bowl and took a bath then put on my dress. I had left my jean jacket at the bar again. Before going to bed I had been listening to the Cocteau Twins, but that morning Bach played through the speaker. I wrote an entry about my novel in my journal. All I have is my heartfelt logic, my honesty, I wrote. It was part of my disposition. But a novel should produce several logics, I thought on my walk to the store. Think of them as procedures. Our eyes scan the line. We assemble the atmosphere in our head in accordance with a sequence of words. The novel may be tested by the number of logics it holds together. Or measured according to the number of people it influences.

I removed a bag of grapes from the shelf and added them to my basket. A man walked by and stared at me in disgust. The flower rattled between my legs. The man and I broke eye contact.

Influence can be measured through pleasure and displeasure, I thought. If the novel exists, if the novel comes into being, it may be measured by the variation in type and number of people it influences. Influence itself occurs through pleasure and displeasure. We can say those who agree with a given novel's argument enjoy the novel whereas those who disagree with it experience displeasure.

I checked my phone and responded to a text.

Influence occurs when we turn toward or away from the novel. Influence is orthogonal, I thought, which made me giggle. Value, what the proselytizers call aesthetic, is produced according to the novel's ability to embrace this turn, to navigate and expand it, to keep movement and propulsion at play. A novel that disturbs, shuns, exposes, violates, or locks out the reader while offering pleasure. I decided that was my goal. I picked up a case of tonic water, allotted myself a discounted kombucha, then headed to the front of the store. Value, in the form of displeasure. A proposition in the form of a flower. In one sense, I was already in my novel. In another, the novel was an object I wanted to become. I thought of Adorno's lectures, the notion that the pianist could merge with the piano. The hands becoming an instrument in lieu of the brain or ear. The human body lending itself as a prosthesis to the piano. The body lending itself as a prosthesis to the concept. Or was I mistaking Adorno for Bernhard, woman for man?

I left the store and carried my groceries home in a paper bag, hugging it close to my chest without using its handles. I wanted to become the dress, its repeating floral pattern. I hated looking at my face, although I knew my face was attractive. It was not my face, but it belonged to me. Or, rather, my face decided how I was perceived. I didn't care how anyone perceived me. No one perceived me in a manner that seemed to reflect who I was. Even to my close friends, I was often something other than myself. It was fine, it didn't bother me. I put the groceries away and sat down on the sofa, to read. I went to the shelf and opened *The Four Fundamental Concepts of Psychoanalysis* by Jacques Lacan. I had made it a practice to read the seminar again every few years, to skim it occasionally. Outside, I noticed the setting sun.

On page 151 of my edition Lacan mentions Chinese astronomy. The Chinese had a perfectly efficient system for predicting diurnal and nocturnal variations. For example, at a very early period, which because of their signifying plotting we can date. Because it is far away enough for the precession of the equinoxes to be marked in it on the figure of the heavens, and because the pole star does not appear in the same place in our time, he said. But then he began to meander. Diurnal and nocturnal variations. Pleasure and displeasure. Valid observations for an efficient system. Was Lacan trying to write a novel as well? In my mind, I saw the pole star shift to the right, saw the figures of the heavens, the precession of the equinoxes — but diagrammatically, in fleshing sketches.

I closed the book and took off my dress. I hung the dress in the closet. By then it was dark outside. Did I want my novel to be valid? Why was everyone talking about authenticity and validity all of a sudden? I remembered the photographs I wrote to you about in Chicago. How I had stood in the doorway without my clothes and lengthened the exposure on the camera to several seconds. The long exposure illuminated the otherwise dark room in the photograph. I didn't use a timed release; I hit the button and walked into the frame in an attempt to wash out the image. Nothing in the photograph resembled or suggested a face. I stood still long enough that my image held, but I looked transparent. I moved my hand in a circle over my genitals until the shutter clicked. I wanted to create a hole in the scenario where my cock would be. I didn't want you to think I was being vulgar. I have a difficult time when I feel exposed. As I have told you, I'm not sure what people see when they see me. Certainly, they don't see me as I see myself. I ended up discarding the images where I didn't face the camera. One of the deleted photographs showed my beard dissolving into a white cloud. I thought about making a triptych. I thought about showing them to you one day. Looking at the pictures changed my mind. I remember I took them because I found myself thinking about suicide in the shower. Not in a dark way, but in the sense that we all die. Perhaps my wish was to be in control of my life and my death. I didn't see anything dark about it. Part of me wants to say this was because I desired to live in a meaningful way. But what life isn't meaningful?

I was writing a novel called *The Cloth* at the time. What would *The Cloth* be about? Who would the novel's main character be? Whose life would I imitate if not my own? I wanted the narrative to unfold less like a story and more like tapestry. I'd decided the best books I'd read never revealed their narrator. Some ended shortly after the narrator disclosed their identity. I almost said after the narrator gave up their identity, but that would have obfuscated what I meant to say. Other times it was someone other than the author who spoke. I wanted to be someone, anyone other than who I was. I figured the novel would allow me to do that. In writing the novel, I would become the novel, I told myself. I remembered when you and I went to an exhibition where one of the artists had sewn her papier-mâché sculptures using magenta thread. I told you how I loved artworks that exposed their stitching, that I wanted to write a novel about a dress decorated with repeating flowers. A novel where a woman discovers a flower growing between her legs and disappears into an article of clothing — a woman who becomes the article itself. It was the only way I could write to you. If I could successfully weave the flower between facts concerning a possible life, its materials and conditions, the events specific to that life, would that be a way of bringing you back? And shouldn't the novel be about you? Wasn't it you who had given me the flower? I had started to think about you all the time. I didn't want to think I was in love with you. I didn't tell my nonexistent husband. I didn't tell my nonexistent husband because I hoped this feeling would go away. I hated the way clothes hung on my body. Perhaps this was why I loved you.

I began to visualize an unoccupied dress adorning a backlit wall when I sat alone and meditated. I meditated because it was a way to observe you in my mind. Distress, Betrayal, Lure, Copycat, Dysphoria, said the journal entry dated 7 November 2017. The striking outline of a body that forms in the crease of a skirt, it continued. Your letter had arrived that morning. Or was it in the afternoon? Maybe the previous evening? I'd been asleep for days. In a sense your letter never arrived. I kept the document sealed inside its envelope. Maybe I would have been easier to love if I were just these words issuing from a void, if I were able to wash myself away as I done in the photograph. At some point in all this pontificating, I realized the novel lived outside the book. That the book was just a doorway or a portal.

I decided to vacate the bedroom and let my novel live there. To give it dimension, volume, space. I understood that the notecards on the wall were the novel's way of establishing contact. I decided to give the cards whatever they needed. I gave them one room in the house at a time. And then I'll invite a few friends over, I thought. But I'd asked them to come sober. That will be the one rule. Because the novel itself is already a drug. I wanted them to experience *The Cloth* without another substance to dull or distort their senses. They could dull or distort their senses once they were here. I would only offer caffeine-free tea, like peppermint or chamomile or turmeric ginger. Nothing that would prevent them from sleep. Because sleep was the only prerequisite. In fact, I would have to ask them to abstain from sleeping for a few days before they entered the room. But, in the end, it wouldn't really matter whether or not they slept. The room would take on the entirety of their sleep. It would take their sleep and replace it with something more composed, more contrapuntal.

FAYE CHEVALIER

feral & not masc enough for a shoulder tattoo

in ceasing, or more folding,

i share a given name

w young Keanu Reeves

in the 1986 feature film *Rivers Edge* &

hiding in a university breakroom,

i tell Rachie tht i have not been eating well,

do not tell her why i have been wearing

long sleeves in the summertime,

& leave to wait for the 21

to take me down to 45th

in this regard,

i mirror young Keanu Reeves in

the 1986 feature film *Rivers Edge*,

as the passage of time

& the urgency of trust

is image-d as a decaying body

& young Keanu Reeves is posited

as both spectator & performer

of the act of rotting

the thrill of losing operations funding;

i will be unemployed come December

the mouse expires on the sidewalk, the flies converge

blood II

what do you call

the only-so-many woundings

tht may befall

a single body?

River Phoenix is long dead,

& as young Keanu Reeves in the 1991

feature film *My Own Private Idaho*,

i live all proof no need,

a loose canvas filled w blood & such,

delighting in facsimile as a

grift-living, coat-slinging pageantry,

e'er ingress-ing, e'er a travesty,

the sequel to a blighted sore; & so,

abandoned by young Keanu Reeves

in the 1991 feature film *My Own Private Idaho*,

i am living to be murdered in Rome—

in two weeks, i will be holding you

for the first time in a year;

my love is a graceless, heaving thing,

a behind-the-scenes calamity—

& long dead River Phoenix

is now long-dead enough

to have lived & died again;

i ache w/o wordings for them—

a killing chasming far far wider than

our final shot of young Keanu Reeves

attending to his father's funeral

in his newly-purchased skin

fantasy football

a living-bruise, a bent but dashing mask
in yr sandy hands, in the stony dark,

time trailing the psycho-(sub)textual milieu
before a young Keanu Reeves
in the 1988 feature film *Permanent Record*,

reason etc a mire-some snare,
wearing skin-for-bones as i am wont to—

the summer-breath
finds me singing "i can pass
the lil wine shop on 43rd
on the way home
w/o seizing now,"

tho the lil-er still tear of nights lost,

simulacrums of far greater despairs

hold close,

&, as young Keanu Reeves in the 1988 feature film

Permanent Record, mourning breathes

(as) breakage in performance,

a living-in the ruin of once-settled

axioms, tho now their ragged legs flay about

& curl over their underbellies,

whilst young Keanu Reeves, splayed about the sand,

cries out for lost love, unanswered—

HARRY JOSEPHINE GILES

ABOLISH THE POLICE

The moon is doing poemy things   & so he takes
a police apart: a police is held   in the silver column
& extracted from himself.   His head, yes, detaches,
but without much drama,   & his arms are peeled with the love
of a Cheestring Original,   cop-strips inspected
by stubbornly poemy moonlight.   The moon spins the dead police
& the dead police uniform   & the moon vanishes all
the dead police to the dead moon sea   where there is quiet.
"I'm sorry," says the moon,   "that I never did this before."
& the people forgive the moon   & let go their poems.

ABOLISH THE POLICE

Before we continue   we must accept "Abolish
the Police" is not   a metaphor, not the silence
from breath to breath, the silence   enclosed
by the colon, not   the spun coin of freedom, nor any
such shifty goalposts, but only   itself, the demand
& its becoming. Here: no police, no prisons,
no psychiatrists, no borders.   The police is not
a metaphor: he is the fist of the state.   Break my mouth!
How could I marshal   metaphor against him, let
words be ought other than beats?   Abolish the Police.

ABOLISH THE POLICE

But of course when I say "Abolish the Police"   I am describing a bird:
bill like a rusted plough,   rump like a loaf of bread,
chin, throat & neck alive   like the mourning surface
of a washing up bowl.   What else could it mean but that this bird's flanks
are expanding   like the breath of a minor mountain, & what else
can describing a bird achieve   but the bloody end of all police?

ABOLISH THE POLICE

& when I read my poem   "Abolish the Police"
to the audience of police,   the police all applaud
& say "Well done,   oh yes, well done,"
their handcuffs rattling   on their little blue plastic chairs.

& when I slide a truncheon   up my lush-lubed rectum
& pogo explaining   how this is the first step
in an ancient ritual   to abolish the police,
the watching police   hum their appreciation
making a cock-handed circle   under my breathless instruction.

"You don't understand,"   I say as I drag
my copper blade   through the neck of a police,
police blood splashing   my polished teeth.
"I mean it. Be gone."   & the police chorus
like a rock   of solan geese,
"Clever, clever, clever."   & I drink up.

ABOLISH THE POLICE

You say that my violence disturbs you.
I press blue fingernails
in an arc around your left nipple
& through, cupping the heart
from above, & this feels
to both of us like truffles melting
against the roofs of our mouths.
"Do you imagine," I say,
"That I am not disturbed?
I wish I could imagine an end
to police untouched by revenge."
"Try harder," you say, slicing a poem
across my palm, a neat cut
that you take into your huge mouth,
eyes sharp with unwanted wealth.

ABOLISH THE POLICE

& we abolish the police by not having sex.
We sit touching skin & speaking
about how we are not having sex, & may
or may not want to have sex, & how
our prickled hair is an object argument,
a vintage alarm clock, an austerity measure.
With each near true word one more
police falls into shining bones.
Our soft parts twitch & when we speak to them
the police bones rattle, looking for love.

ABOLISH THE POLICE

Yes, toy police drop from my   tongue. Cops march
my full throat. The cop band   twangs my chords,
slaps my teeth, bubbles spit   into horns, wires amps
to my pons. Like any voice I   voice cop song.
Like any body tiny police are   blood to my brain,
smoke to my lungs. Like you,   before I swallow I chew.

ABOLISH THE POLICE

So we take a single police   into our bed & hold him:
his great round helm is rough   on my tits,
his long lean legs   jerk in your lap, his tears
trinkle between us,   silvering the sheet.

So of course we give comfort.   His shake rocks the head
board. We offer our love & our fingers   to lick till his yowl
is only a far off drill. Every police   merits the gift
of your stretchmarks, the guff   of my oxters, our dirt.

So of course we forgive. It takes   but a sound. My lips
to his temple yield new life.   It takes but his true
& godsworn will, & every police   is owed a second roll.
The three of us warm in our grace like   parbaked baguettes.

Of course we dunk our teeth into his neck.   Of course
we drag vein from bone, lung from chest.   Of course
we repaint the walls with his grease   & add liver
to the shelf. What else   did he think was the smell.

ABOLISH THE POLICE

& here is the medal   hung round your neck.
"You did it," I declare with Olympic weight.   "You abolished."
"No you!" you say, "You!"   & from behind my ear
pop a second coin & string   more triumph to me.
We pass the day passing prizes   between us, ramming
our room   with great mounds of win. "You!" I say,
"You!" you say, & under the gold   their guts, our uniforms.

ABOLISH THE POLICE

So here in my bed the police are abolished.   No fluids,
no settlement: only a duvet   like warm snow, & only
the desire for no police & the actual   no police
& your morning   wood at rest on my crack.

But police come through the crack   in the blind,
bronze shields bearing   the smile of a vicious day,
in which abolition is teething   at the buttered toast of death,
& there was always death in the bed,   & the sun clears her throat.

HAZEL AVERY

SISTER CITY

sister cities suggest a sort of sisterly similarity, as in, a correspondent sameness sistering grasses, cities, fish and piss, an axis of sisterness, if you wish, which secrets itself in the way a sister seems to see another, distant, show- ing seams of self-sistering and saying a sister as such or, suggesting that this sister and that one touch, so sisters seeking sameness wish to see a self in someone else, a secret city sister nestled in the grasses cities sub-sume and subsist upon, grasses missing, as it is, from any sort of citied sisterness, which is more cyst than sister, which cisterns sisters like fish to pitch fits and twist sister wrists til sisters seek to see self not in distances but miss-ing- ness, to wit, sister cities sister city sisters, to city a sis-ter is to seek the piss in the fish, that is, to seek the sticky stench of sisterness and to leave herself where she wish to twist a nest of sisterness and stick it in the secret stash of grasses sisters smash into the cracks of sister states, to distance the wishing in spite of the missing it, to suppose a distant sister knows the flows of sisterness the same as she, to make it seem to be as if the city spreads in spaces of the sisterless, the emptied scenes of sisters seeming something else, when city sisters know how sister cities sever fish from rivers and sisters from fish, that a city as a sisterness renders other sisters missing, optimistically, or else useless in their separateness, absent from the cities of sisters seeing sameness in the distance but still secretly seeking sweetness, a missing as a kind of kiss, a seeing sisterness without saying sister is, this is to say, city sister seeks same, while the cityless stay secret in their missing- ness, a sister can't sister what she can't see, sister stay, sis- ter city wishes only witnesses, she says as much, sister city slyly offers touch, to sip the cups full of sisterness after filling such, sister stay, you sister this way, the city sistered you, only emptiness and sisterless sleep outside the citied sister, stay, sister, such sisterless spaces suck the sister from your sister too, the city sister saves your sister skin from letting secrets in, stay, sister, city sister wishes it.

piss sister

i fear there is
something in us
    that lets us be
    sisters that lets
us be useless
sisters a kind
    of touching that
    we have forgotten
how to touch
a way that we
    touch already that
    we have forgotten
the touching of
there is some
    thing that runs
    thru me that
runs thru you
too and it is
    not a pretty
    thing sister
        i wish it
        were a pretty thing
    sister but it
    is not a pretty

thing and i
fear there is
        something we
        left in the fields
                of us the fields
                we forgot of us
        i wish it were
        pretty sister
but there is
something we
        are missing and
        it is not coming
                back to us
                sister we have
        to live this way
        now this is how
we live it is
not a pretty
        thing i fear i
        have broken some
                thing i know i
                have never
                        broken but i
                        still fear having
                broken it there
                is something

        missing for us
        sister are there
kinds of sisters
we do not know
        how to touch
        is this what
                we are missing

i have forgotten
what we are
missing and
it is not
a pretty thing
something is
a pretty thing
out there in
the field sister
yes the field
sister who i
remember now
she is a pretty
thing so far
distant from
us sister i
fear that i
no longer carry
the knowing
of
the field sister
close to me
i have forgotten
how to carry
it is not a
pretty thing
but i know
where to find
a pretty thing
sister can we
remember an
unfielded sister
ness sister can
we go to the

field can we
please i want
to remember
a pretty thing
i want to touch
a pretty thing
to my unpretty
thing sister i
want to hold
a pretty thing

in my unpretty
hands i will
be so careful
with the pretty
thing sister i
want to hold it
what do you
mean there are
no pretty things
left where did
they go what did
you do with them
i just want to
hold one to
hold a pretty thing
i'll be careful
with the pretty
thing i promise
just this once
please i promise

HOLLY RAYMOND

Secret Mission Orders for Goblin Romantic:

The dream is to be moved by anything at all. By this Garfield fan-comic in which Jon collapses on the kitchen floor, linked triangles and hoops painted onto a wall stretching three storefronts, mannequins in full-plate clutching their scabbards, folded t-shirts, the shape of a dreadnought through glass wearing all denim. Pass through a cloud of vape smoke in the canned isinglass department, exit bawling at the beauty of all manifest creation. You will aspire to enter into labor translucent, like a paraffin sheet, wet and flammable, light passing thru shape. Alchemy is based on such a fluidity of exchange-- all my affect splattering out into the public sphere, cathecting onto every measly beloved thing. You are to be compensated unfairly for your infinite labor, work your little mitts to the marrow scraping every feel from every surface, squirreling away a bit here, a bit there, to balance the scales, to furnish your home with objects of attention, popcorn chicken festering under plastic, somebody else's keys-- goblin in the streets, bugbear in the sheets, & under the paving stones, defeat. This will all be according to plan.

In Goblin Mall, still melancholic, inexplicably, still reedy and thick with unchecked pips in teeth, still gnawing the fibers from the goblin bills, still holding that nothing up to the light and muttering. Such discontent to see the star twist out of view and know the malls shall die anon anon. How the bridge shudders against the bridge, and the bridge in turn goes coughing shyly. You, paid in double exposure, walking as it were on beetleshells. Say to the vast red eye overhead, you don't know, you only work here, and after work, sleep in the model beds (for fun). It's mostly pretense. Sun thru the fake palms and skylights. Total carapace to cup you in, o in a worker's armor, the vile smell of it.

In love with product, steal you what you vend. Peddle as a mediator, touch a stranger's hand to pass what's craved, squander, your smoke breaks are infinite; watch tapes to lazily know each name as a grunt or a whistle, pockets fat with surplus, fingers deep in the salad bar, gloves off, you are married to my crime-habitus. Your earbuds and chargers and red vouchers, slipped into my burlap sack, will someday come gaily to call me mom.

In Goblin Mall all the flowers are cops. They sing your title. All the birds are cops too. Every beautiful thing you remember as named from a poem-- that's cops baby. I know not where you go to, hands in the apron,head low thru every hanging garden, the cars for kids wobbling on their motors and tithe,
the perfume of the dogwoods calling you to your arrest,
calling your wage out as Nemesis in absentia,
unstoppable and demure and 10,000% fired

One or Several Goblin Girl Workers Dreaming in Unison of the Mothman:

In my dream its tongue was colloidal silver.
In my dream it was a hunter on the earth.
In my dream the bridges rumble not in fracture but in desire.
In my dream we all tied flashlights to helium balloons to frighten the townsfolk.
In my dream the Mothman took me in its maw like a cough drop.
In my dream a great machine called the Steam Man of the Prairie levels all the walls, but when all hope seems lost a different albeit very similar machine called the Steam Man of the Plain comes charging in and restores them.
We all watched helpless but knew the Mothman had a plan for all things that would shake out ok.

In my dream the Mothman held the code to pop the till.
In my dream the Mothman barges in at closing with no shoes and no shirt.
In my dream the Mothman tips in feathers encased in amber.
In my dream I was slain by the beat of its wings in the middle of karaoke, I stood there in front of all my dead friends singing a beautiful girl group bop called "Tokyo Grifter," the sun shone over and around me, gleaming, and when I woke I cried that it didn't exist nor I to sing it or nab it up in vanishing.
In my dream its shirt is too little.
I dream it glows like a bicycle reflector.
I dream the vortex is spinning closer.
In my dream the moon turns around and it has the Mothman's face. It winks and blows smoke from its great cigar, obscuring the city. The people smash windows. Everybody coughs for hours.

In my dream I am its wife. I have it made. I sit by the pool drinking my drink and dragging my green toes through the shallow end. It travels for work. An empty instant pot and a big brown paper bag full of vegetables and meat.

I am noble in inactivity. I await the Mothman's coming.

In my dream we duck beneath a table to avoid it.
In my dream it is bossed around intolerably.
In my dream instead of money it strokes our palms gently and shows us in its big red eye some premonition of our future happiness, and in exchange we fill its canvas bag with bottles of soda, green and red radishes, soap, and ginger.

In my dream, money, but with the Mothman's face on one side and a crude map of the mall on the other. It says "1,000,000,000 Mothbux" and can't buy much of anything.
In my dream its swordplay cuts me down to size in the field of love (primrose, poppies, etc.).
In my dream the Mayor, swimming up through the wreckage, grasping towards something.
In my dream mothdust snuffs me to a further sleep, behind the anchor store, under the clover of the hills.
I dream of stress corrosion cracking in an eyebar on a suspension chain.
I dream of acting up all level 99 cut out against the sun and auspicious, of a limit break, of a soft stat cap.
In my dream the Mothman crashes in with a gun and we huddle idly in the walk-in freezer.
In my dream it lists its demands for eighteen days and eighteen nights without stopping for breath.

I dream of grinding mobs until it's boring. I'm given a free longbow but I throw it out. It's garbage.
In my dream it never ends but keeps crashing into some civic flame or another, burning with a deep howl, pressing its huge form against the bunker walls, against the plate windows.

In my dream the going out of business sale is permanent and the savings live forever,
like God does, a thing in a white plastic bag, a fake happiness, but still[1]

1. *Correction!* False. Every goblin has the same dream, the same dream every night. They dream of killing their bosses. In their dreams they advance with giant red hedge-trimmers. They advance with TNT sticks like piano keys arranged inside their mouths. In their sleep they make their move with the mallet or the anvil or the conveyor belt with buzz-saws attached. The mall is on fire. It is tied to the train-tracks and the train is coming. Or, in some versions, the mall blooms anew, a million pale blue flowers exploding from the meadow.

Bosses chopped up for scrapple. Boss soup. Boss cake. In the cold Yukon they look at the boss and the boss' head is a big cooked turkey. They all consume the boss' boiled shoe, with boiled boss-foot soft inside. A million goblin hands on a million goblin pitchforks. The crowd has their back. The crowd's hand pulls the lever with the smoothness of a single hand, in the dreams of goblins. When the bridge falls their eyes pop out of their sockets and their tongues flop down the corridors like long wet carpets, and their voices say *awooga*, steam comes out of their ears, this is a shorthand that means they're happy or kind of turned on. It's known that each one smiles in its sleep to the melody of gigantic violence but what can you do? Anyway, so, that's what goblins dream about.

By the Gayborhood Shake Shack I Sat Down and Wept

hold a magic whip up and snap it
take out all the windows
I explain to 80,000 totally asleep-style swains
the way things are going to be
I am stomping on the head of my own vocation
they are staring impolitely at my alchemy tits
and forgetting what my name is
no
I'm kidding
I'm nice   I'm nice

let us teach one another like
we're robbing a bank,
those of us already married
hollowing our bodies out,
filling in wet space with
some stranger's creature teeth
I encourage you to walk out,
I encourage it, oh, I encourage
your failure to mention
my little legs ambling
up stairs in novel sheaths,
this skirt
with black flowers on it,
my tedious red innards

on my office door the name of an evil magician
expelled from the academy, by me, a hero.
an evil magician with a haircut I hate,
destroyed with daggers.
let all my students become assassins
or sob like bastards
braced against the skeleton of news
let snipers carry my fake coquette
ass up to heaven on magic bolts
let them all skip class, what
do I care, let them tear up the pavement,
eat sweets dandy from deep in the trash,
for free,
I will give you all an A, for free,
while gently touching the poof of my hair
like a very mean widow
at a very small grave

all alone downtown and free from
all my obligations, knocked to shit by
wind and socked in the eye
dumb ingenue of vortex I
lift the hem of my skirt up--
spiders everywhere!
I may be mostly vegetarian,
but here I am, weeping,
with my fist inside the carrion,

dragging my fries through the wreckage and the mustard seed--
alive, tbh, in a dream of gentleness,
melting away like a jellyfish mating,
I will not die in this town without
some other mammal's hot blood
in my mouth

IAN KHARA ELLASANT

let me tell: you Diana

i'm tired of fighting you Diana
about the stories we will tell
about who you say you are still
girl you or still me no
Diana listen
girl you gotta let me
let me go
boy
thinks i'm trying
thinks i'm eager
Diana let me tell you i ain't

which is the better question
no girl you get real
ask the easier question
which is more:
how much we are or
how much we are not the same
how nothing and everything is
boy and *and* or *or* girl you
are nothing and everything you
still the same Diana listen
girl you turning boy
shake him loose or
shake me loose Diana
loose of girl and loose of boy

girl you   gotta let me
                  let me go
                          boy
thinks i'm crawling toward his face
thinks i'm spreading my shoulders
into the corners of his broad back
Diana let me tell you   i ain't

are you kidding me Diana

do you love well do you
the hard first of love the hard fist
and we don't say yes
don't say no
do say *what difference does it make*
do say *it won't change nothing*
who are we kidding then
do break our backs our hearts
do bloody our knuckles digging
an escape an entrance
a grave six years deep
between yes and no

the hard first of love the hard fist
the first night defines us finds us as we
tumble out onto 4th ave hold up
adobe walls stucco chainlink until daybreak
stumble stupid into some feeble cling
confess some crack-laced thing like love
mumble some thing some seething little thing
like a secret we wrench
from between each other's clenched teeth
give it here
like so what whatever anyway

like we stub our toes on a rock in the way

pick it up and hurl it at the moon

like we are mad about it   somehow

we are a pair now

we are sway and slur in june

go ahead and do your work now   i say

go ahead and do your worst stuff now   just get it

out of the way   so

you punch me in the stomach

just haul off and slug me in the gut

double me   over

are you kidding me Diana   well anyway

i laugh about it for years

JACKIE ESS

AUTUMN LEAVES

Give yourself to me in a single word,
Whatever's the second to come to mind.
I miss you the way you were at first.
You've changed some, even for the better. That's fine.

Invisible acrobat, spry leaper over rooftops,
I followed you in a secret revery.
This was something like the way we dreamed we'd dance.
Psychic parkour, a way to wriggle free.

I met you in the Autumn of the year I discovered love.
It must have been about the third or fourth time.
In seasonless Seattle. Not daring to aspire.
I gasped for breath. You threw me a line.

There was a rumor about the rain, so we huddled indoors.
Suffocating crush, too many to a room.
These girls are fucked up, man. I'm telling you.
So the lists. We're both on them now. It's all true.

Then politics, demanding a cock in every pot
or, barring, a feather in every cap.
A universal quill. A substitute field.
I wounded you there. & was wounded. We healed.
But you didn't call me!

WEATHER

I have the sound of your voice, the music you showed me,
& the thought that we would have hated one another,
& I mean really hated, had we met when we were young.
Come to think of it, that's actually how it happened.

But I get to know you anyway, because we both have presence.
An occult sense everywhere of your having passed through.
There's a flash in the spirit, as impersonal as powder,
or unusual weather. There are these auroras & so on,

Slight incense on a frozen wind, then melt.
Ice-bergs peeling off from the part of life that matters.
Which is the massive. Those are the rules, that's the prompt,
As I reminded anyone who'd listen.

JAMIE TOWNSEND

SPIT ON YOUR GRAVE

There's a bruise above both eyes

Luxury queen smirking on the chopping block

Valerie and her week of wonders

Soft lighting and gossamer sheets

There's a lip bleeding for your fantasy

Cream we washed in pulled from a tit

There's the impression of a hand

Furious with desire and strident

Not bashful, meek or wilting

On the cheek I ripped off the dream

Spent two stacks on a makeup bag

The gore we splashed around in

Demure morse code for personal space

I don't even need this skin

A barb, a knife, an exfoliating scrub

There's a base coat smeared everywhere

Dripping pestilence and honeyed bile

Our smize a black Cheshire cat

A fluffer drowning the room in red

There's pus along the nail-bed a French tip

Agony aunt, inspiration and soul twin

A cleanser applied at night

To sleep with this plan of waking to a new face

The cut, the bruise, spitting up the scum, I will

ENERGY VAMPIRE

Destroyer tries to sing through Kara Walker's eyes

The stiff wand beneath his shadow work blurring any sense of subtlety

Shaking our head to a blunt obfuscation we agree it's hard to make out

Then probably too easy when we stop fucking around

I'm studying how to dress well, its louche anxiety

Stripping from it what I can

An ingenue spitting up a stolen music

A soft kind of love that does no justice to the chorus

That keeps being erased by our singular desire

To be free, 'without your neck to kiss, I was thrown to the night'

I read this like sucking blood or quoting Celine Dion

An irresponsible need to slip into the cloud of unknowing one more time

All these young dudes are trying to tug at my heartstrings

While they spread their legs I stiffen into

White columns of a mausoleum our love mistakes for authenticity

Violence is full of the shape our art steps into

Inadequate space of the we I'm trying to reclaim as legion swirls through

An army not the orgy I imagined

Night is a forest tugging at our loins

And the blush feels resonant, like a drum head rasped

With innumerable waves embracing and pulling us away

To a place where eyeless things love us with their whole heart

We can't see them yet feel this is what we've always wanted

JAYSON KEERY

Me Problem

Well, that was a negative sexual experience.
Had sex with a person who said they were non-binary
but was shocked to discover my tiny penis.

I spoon my trans friends for comfort and
have an idea! Let's all give each other tattoos.
They'll say T4T, except, I propose,
we get two tea bags tangled.
Code.

Not days after T4T branding my skin,
I promptly have sex with
an openly cis-identifying woman.
First time for me,
if you can believe.
Something in me still scared
to be gay and okay in my
~cute~ new masculinity.

She kisses me at midnight.
It's New Years and I hardly know her.

Someone tries calling at midnight and that someone is dying.
I don't pick up.

New year new me.

She asks if I got a car to fuck in.
I offer a house and she scratches
the back of my head
the whole way home
long nails with the gay ones cut
short is hot. I'd do it too,
but apparently I need
all of them. Working my way in.
About to ask consent to be fisting,
she beats me to it,
she unbuckles my fitbit,
she slings it off,
she fucking threw it,
she fucking threw my fitbit.
Have to wait until the next morning
alarm goes off
to find it
she says
"I don't want that in me."

I have no way to track
how long I didn't sleep.
Perhaps worried
I dream of only loving cis women.
Perhaps worried
I came in someone's boobs.
First time for me.
This time my tiny penis
the one in shock.

Just because someone's femme
doesn't mean I have to be butch to it.

That's a me problem.
She's deeply gay and I like it.

She talks about another poet writing poetry about her.
I tell her I probably won't.

JESI GASTON

HARPO'S BROTHERS

From the heights of incoherence comes his double to his place in those depths of lucid living, at which he asks himself, quiet even in himself like a thousand angel's wings in flight, which double this was now, noting, quieter and remote, that like any good double his came in two, like still more wretched angels descending with his double the thought came that never would the both set down in one, and never would he have to see how different either was from the other nor gawk empty-headed and gracious at what that meant with that innocent and reckless gaze he was stuck with and at which, he knew in the part of his chest that was quieter still, where with that stillness of soul he could know things, whichever double was coming down would scoff. He fixed his coat up. He dusted nothing off himself, but made the motions, then fixed his coat up, and figured other busy work to occupy his hands. In elegant galumphing from roofs on roofs upon him, just the one, and all that quiet of the soul he knew was counterposed to the noise his presence wrought focused on the flight through which the double danced as the dance was ending and, setting down right next to him he saw the one that came. He beat the tattoo over his heart, which had been singing itself into a stupor, and the patter of his hand set him at something like an ease, and ready for what it was was asked of him.

HARPO'S FROG

That the frog of crumpled leather, bashed against the wind these many years, looks so brittle on his head, with its skin so much like cardboard, through which anyone, at the right angle driven against it's impossibly thin surface, could push their fingers – no matter how gingerly their press nor how daintily their fingers' masses went and were – even by accident and not excluding the foregoing, it warrants saying, could anyone just stab this frog right through and break it – and likewise could, considering its lot and the agony that accompanies, be so long quiet and appreciative and proud, that all of this he considered often, even as he threw it and he rung it in his hands, and some or another strong man often threw it from his head and stomped it in a cruelty he would match, and more, with all the light dropped on him from on high, that even when pain and pain and pain ran through his mind and, only natural to a mind like his, he knew the frog to be the one to run it, being so close to and above his brain, yet still he felt a stronger loyalty to him, frog, than any other he had ever known – that this all could be true, and was, was nothing to him, as everything.

HARPO'S MOMENT IN THE SUN

That *Monkey Business* ultimately sits, a monument to Harpo's grace, in unearned obscurity, underneath the rubble of *Duck Soup's* last act – that bouffon's paradise of misery, that polyphony of inchoate yaps, a song from the loins and the bowels of the demiurge he called alternately "double" and "brother" – gives less pause to Harpo, who has no room for pause and no insides to stop up, living as he does a life comprised of one fluid motion, one line not cut into discrete sections, making for no stumbling of his feet beneath him and fewer thoughts – of which none have ever wholly lacked doubt, so of course he went without those – than to the minor demon himself, that one who knows inadequacy and how to make like that gnashing he does with his teeth is genuine – a distinctly modern wink at the gap between the voice and the situation that does well to conceal the grinding underneath that's as true as the right to self determination of all peoples so long as they aren't women – as well he knows jealousy, none of which so much as brushed against Harpo, who knows only the one fluid motion – an edict against memory and a better thing to worship if ever there was in him the capacity for either at the start, a thing so powerful and true that to follow it and follow it true, like only he could only do, renders the rest, and all the words, against him, such that what preceded and the following comes not as statements but a speculation as to what the impossible insides of a thing like him would be if they were in the way we understand things; a nothing for the nothing was his prayer comprised of nothing maintaining as always it does in him the positive nothing, an indetermination for which Groucho could only wish. But what does Harpo know? Where does Harpo's mind – or what we approximate as such in order to carry on believing we can know or just grow towards knowing him – go? The man approaching roughly, pulling at his arm, tugging roughly – what was it he wanted, after all? Harpo clearly can't remember – said something – and so, unbeknownst to him, willed an impossible moment – to the vacant-smiled clown, who looked so small in all his layered rags, propped against a brick wall that looked rattier still than his get up and curiously of a part with only him even in the dirt thoroughfare, the gist of which went, "What are you, busy?" to which he had to nod, dumb and beckoned toward this action, "You holding the building up?" to which he was bound all the more emphatically to nod, the providence inside him inspired and him not unaware of what would come, so that when his nod subsided and the man pulled him roughly away, the cacophony of bricks against the dirt, the thunderousness and the drowned out neighs of horses and screams of men in well-formed, expensive hats, was a fact like the Sun or Groucho's grief, both of which shined on him, then, the queer Diogenes.

JESSICA BET

DALMATIAN PEOPLE

for Bernadette Mayer's Utopia

Who flees
the Bank of society?

That Frenchwoman
Gauguin.

Who chronicles
the groveling shame
and disgrace?

That Frenchwoman
Duras.

Who flees
the State, the men's club
and who stays

and goes to bed
to service it tomorrow
in low-wage white labor
uniform?

Who awaits
to wake
in yogic pose
to uphold the State
with straight
partners.

They were straight all along.
As their life circles down
the wedding band
like toilet water.

Tell me to stop
when I touch nerves.
To bide time and
stay here and bathe
in warm frog's water,
as you unlock. The water
warm but
never boils.

*

Who
among the hundred
will guard your Life?

If I bury you in wisdom now,
tomorrow we'll be gone,
that you may breathe.
Not to crack your egg.

But do not stop.
You should find out
like the floating turtle,
that is fast but slow,
which one
will guard you.

JIMMY COOPER

Untitled

DENIM CHERUBIM CURLS OVER COLLAR
CHOKING CHANGELING DRINKING COORS LIGHT
LAUGHING LIGHTING UP SMILING BITTER
"I'VE GOT THIS BODY— I'VE GOT THIS BODY—"
LIGHTER THAN EVERYTHING HEAVIER THAN NOTHING
PLAYING NERVOUSLY WITH THREAD MUMBLING
FEET UP ON THE COUCH IN RUSTY BOOTS—
FEEL A LITTLE RUSTY MYSELF LITTLE LONG-LEGGED
RUNNING, RUNNING, & NOW
HOLY IT ANNOUNCES LIKE A NEON CHURCH SIGN
BUT NOTHING LIKE THAT AT ALL.
I THINK I'D BE OKAY IF I DIDN'T FEEL THIS WAY.
ONCE I GOT AN EXTRA HOUR, FREE TIME.
NOW IT GOES ON FOREVER TOO MUCH BUT COME ON,
PUSH ME A LITTLE HARDER ANYWAYS.
I DREAM OF GETTING INTO A FISTFIGHT FOR THE LENGTH OF THE SONG.
YOU KNOW THE TUNE.
I'D NEVER TAKE MY RINGS OFF JUST FOR YOU.
DON'T WORRY, DEAR, IT'S JUST A SCUFFLE.
JUST NOTHING, I SWEAR.
MAYBE ANGELS.
MAYBE YOU.

i am really, truly in this bitch poem

got my shirt off skinny dipping—
im bleeding in the pool but its alright
dont often have my tits out like that but
i was fifteen? sixteen?
the night before my first big pridefest &

I'm here, I'm here, I'm here
I am inhabiting my body
I am really, truly in this bitch!

& the next morning bleary-eyed we dress to the nines &
i see a boy in leather for the first time
& i know that will be me someday
but first become pretty vacant
choke on my own hipbones

I am going to kill the Presidents of the United States of America
for writing Lump which I will never listen to again.

instead lose my virginity
1000 times
pick up a few bruises cool river stones & pray.
he will listen & not reply as always & i will die
tagging void tagging coffins & loose safety pins

For an anarchist I sure am an attention whore.
Nothing to lose but my chains.
I've come to like the camera.

I'd like to make a cameo as something more than what I was back then.
Please be gentle as you tie it— I'm all yours—
but—
but—

I was bleeding.
Never got used to it.
And now/I won't.

JOSÉ DÍAZ

Yes a conversation

J: I don't think I'll ever be good enough. I don't even know for what. I just won't ever be good in a holistic sense. I'm good at kissing and I'm good at crying and I'm good at falling in love. I think that's it. Wait, I'm also good at remembering my dreams after I wake up. When you see me in your dreams, is it good?

Yes. You are completely different in my dreams. You walk around with a bag of mangoes and Hass avocados. You bite into your fruits at the end of every sentence you say. When you speak, green and yellow chunks fly out and hit my face.

J: Do you think I'll die alone, in a compromised position, with my dick out in my hand, facing the ocean? I wonder how many miles deep sunbeams go into the water. When you find my body, will you dump me into the sea and make sure I sink deep, but not so deep that the sun never hits me?

Yes. I'll throw you over my shoulders and push your body into the waves like flotsam. I'll dive down with you until I find the perfect spot. It won't be so hard to do; I don't think sunlight can swim far.

J: If I could, I would dress more... androgynous. Look trans, look feminine. When I reference my dick in my writing, I get concerned people will leave thinking I'm a man. My last lover wanted me to be a man. Did you want me to be a man?

Yes. Before you told me you weren't a man, I already knew. I don't remember what I thought you were before. Not a man. In the future, I thought I'd be a better person where that didn't matter, and it was only about love.

J: Will we get drunk together again? The two us vomiting into the same bush like before? Is there someone new who waits outside the shower when you go to wash away your confusion? Do they step in and scrub your back like I used to?

Yes. We can drink together whenever you want. Or whenever I miss you. The only person waiting outside my shower is the beautiful man you imagine. He might as well be real. You can make him out so clearly, even from behind all the steam.

J: I like to imagine you in the world without me. I see you shirtless, how you prefer to be, standing over the kitchen counter mixing mac and cheese. You're wearing a silly pinwheel hat and shaking your ass to a Destiny's Child song. Do you ever imagine me in the world without you?

Yes. You are barefoot, stepping over jagged pebbles reaching for the makeshift scythe you keep by the fruit trees. You are slicing off part of a branch so the fruits will fall. The sunlight splits after hitting the hanging lemons. Some have fallen on their own, now spotted with rings of mold. You cradle a batch of ripe ones, careful not to spill any. But still, one escapes to roll across the dirt.

J: Do I pick it up?

Yes. This time, you dig your nails into the skin.

JOSHUA JENNIFER ESPINOZA

CONFESSIONAL POEM

The day the government announced a plan to strip away even more basic human rights from trans people, I hooked up with someone I met on Tinder. I'd been rejected that afternoon by another who'd referred to me as "So beautiful" but unmatched when I told her about my gender situation. The person I ended up meeting, on the other hand, was cool with it. She let me know while we were fucking that she had a thing for "chicks with dicks," conceiving of us as "the best of both worlds". I promised myself I would process this another time. As she rode me, she said she was pretending my dick was hers and she was fucking me with it. Reader, I was extremely into this. I was even more into it when she flipped me over and starting grinding herself against my ass. "Oh my god I'm gonna cum," she moaned and I felt her warm trickle down my crack and soak my little hole and I could hardly stay inside my body. Afterward, I snuggled my head against her chest while she talked about a desire to explore her masculine side, thanking me for giving her the chance to express it. I ran my fingers through her closely-cropped hair, stroking the little buzz of sideburn next to her gorgeous metal-adorned ear. "I see it," I said, tilting my face to meet her gaze. "I see you." She pulled me closer into her arms and sighed against the back of my neck. Later, while saliva dripped from above onto my waiting tongue, I wondered what it would mean to see myself. What I might be.

When I finished swallowing her spit I went to say something, but she didn't hear me. "You're beautiful," was all she could repeat.

"So beautiful".

SONNET FOR THE INTR
TO CRITICAL THEORY
PROFESSOR WHO MAD
HER NEGATIVE FEELIN
ABOUT TRANS PEOPLE
PERFECTLY CLEAR
AT MULTIPLE POINTS
DURING EVERY LECTU
AFTER I CAME OUT TO
HER IN THAT FUCKING
GUT-CHURNING “PLEA
CALL ME BY MY CHOSE
NAME AND NOT THE O
ON THE ROSTER” EMAI
I’D HAVE TO SEND OUT
ALL MY INSTRUCTORS
EVERY TERM

She finds tenuous ways of working it
in; *So yeah, because of post-modernism*
men can now decide to call themselves women—
She shrugs and she frowns. I don't give a shit,
or try not to at least. I'm here to get
an education. In the email I'd asked gen-
tly if I could be referred to as Jen-
nifer. One word reply: *Fine.* I don't get
why someone would be driven to such great
lengths to embarrass a student. Me, with
my baby-trans lipstick and belief that
all people deep down contain love and truth.
Trans is the same as chopping off an arm,
she says. But I'm all arms, lost in the swarm.

JOSS BARTON

pink_sissy

A photo of pink_sissy posted on IG when she wasn't looking: Bitch had just started 'mones and her hair was wrapped in silk mod pattern scarf, and child she reads me in the name of Lazarus! Said she was taking out the trash like the fleets in my waste can like the anon cum loads oozing out my ass!

The word ode feels too soft for the cocks she memorized in typewriter font Craigslist ads plastered along South Grand. Left on Chippewa, swerve on a tranny memory, take a right at the cursed intersection at Gustine where cars & cargo trucks full of beer soaked day laborers meet in glass ridden amazement, roll past the flats of immigrants growing young peppers in front lawn gardens and ruddy women woven in rainbow cloth on faded brick stoops, readjust a chubby cock in mesh basketball shorts as you park the HONDA, pass through the storm door:
KNOCK TWICE:
ASK IF TRANSSEXUAL DYSTOPIA IS HOME:
ASK IF ALL THE FULLY FUNCTIONAL TRANNY TOPS HAVE MOVED TO CLEVELAND:
ASK IF THE DOLLS WERE ABANDONED BY THE ANAL SEX GODS WHOSE PUNISHMENT ARE MEN WHO DON'T RIM!

HOLY MOTHERS! PROTECT US IN THIS TIME OF HOMOSEXUAL BANALITY!

DO NOT TRUST THE GAY WHITE MAN RUNNING FOR PRESIDENT!

DO NOT TRUST CIS SAVIORS!

DO NOT TRUST WHITE WOMEN WHO DO NOT LISTEN TO BLACK WOMEN!

AND DON'T EVER FUCKING TRUST TRADE WITH YOUR CAR!
AMERICA! MOTHER OF MULES! QUEEN OF HOLLOW VIRTUE!

Sing us a song! Scratch the bowels and paint flowers with the blood! Tell us the world is beautiful on the other side of barbed wire fences where owls hang executed by divine destiny. Rip the sheet metal off my back, straddle the bones of my satin bedpost, saturate Saturday sins with seroconversion-sonnets, and pink_sissy crushing a roach beneath concrete bitten pumps. See the guts, white and soft, smell the stink of insect brains wiped across the sole as a site for parasites or the kind of tongue that roots into a man's asshole searching for real lies. Another filter of static stars in our hair: another roadside motel to pull double dates in: another anointed ass to breed: another client to fist: another question of what it means to be alive in this world, at this time, surrounded by these horrors: another movie to check into the viewing queue: another strain to mutate: another world app fucked and wiped with snot rag cocks slimy and pulsating and our lips whore neon as we enter the temple, stoned, burning the foreheads of faggot elders, pumping our transsexual cocks and cumming on the money tables. The good old boys play Def Leppard's Hysteria as they suck us off in their pick up trucks. They send pink_sissy texts of dick pics and coke mirrors begging to breed her, their incessant snaps remind her that everyone wants a whore, but no one wants to wake up next to one.

The problem for many old guard gays is that trannies are now living the lives that dangerous faggots used to live which in part produces both jealousy and resentment that the dolls are more subversive more radical more gorgeous and more cock hungry than they ever were: SO IT IS WHAT IS ALWAYS IS: TRANS MISOGYNY FROM BITTER QUEENS: How fucking typical that right now it's trans women of color, BLACK & BROWN TRANS WOMEN, who must grin until our lips bleed as we watch our rainbow peers pat themselves on the backs for their tranny flag avatars while simultaneously refusing to fiercely protect and nourish us: We get to see how much our lives really mean as we count the hashtags against the job offers, the HIV infections against the second/third/fourth/fifth chances, the willingness to let us bleed out our political traumas on stages and screens for THEIR HEALING against the bruises on our bodies or the obituaries they never read.

pink_sissy sheds the skin off her nipples like human scales, wraps her heart together with a bouquet of transsexual molting, bites the flesh, rips the ligament memories, warms a nest of cellophane with the light of electricity against a black sky stabbed with white pins poked through the lining of night silk. Haunted bodies buried beneath this estrogen soaked skin brittle nails chipped on the teeth of transsexual ghosts wailing for freedom or a chance to try it over again to re-wind the tape and roll the dice and this time aim for healing or heaven or anywhere but eternally stuck on this elevator to Human Resources.

She keeps trying to write something better than these shemale Pornhub poems. She sits down to type a title: NO MORE DEATH POEMS: tries to find sentences symbolism stanzas about absolutely anything: rows of lines on watermelon seeds spit from the wet pink lips of milkweed boys smoking pot in red florescent bar lights: prose on Detective Pikachu, pisco sours, pine trees in June, potted plants in macrame webs: Haikus on the Holy Trans Mothers: Sylvia Sylvester Marsha Ms. Major Ms. Leon TS Madison Tracey Norman Candis Cayne Candy Darling CeCe McDonald Crystal LeBeija Laverne Cox Trace Lysette Flawless Sabrina Van Barnes Bamby Salcedo Maria Roman Passion Principle Janet Mock: BUT ALL THAT COMES OUT ARE THE AGES & NAMES & HOMETOWNS & NAMES & HASHTAGS & NAMES & CAUSES OF DEATH & NAMES & FUNERAL FUNDS & NAMES & WHERE THEIR BODIES & THEIR DREAMS WERE FOUND & THEIR FUCKING NAMES but the grim rhythm of reaper repetition fades into white noise and she knows this is what an epidemic sounds like: dead static silence running across the black nothingness of Arkansas Delta as she drives out of Memphis: How can anyplace be so pitch black? So empty? No trees or stars or the whir of moths or the screams of locusts or the choir of crickets or the soul catching of whippoorwills or the howls of coyotes or the chirps of rain frogs? Every rattle and bump on this goddamn road reminds her how fucked we will be if she breaks down here. We left the last gas station a good hour ago and there's only the white eyes of a semi-truck in the desolate distance floating in more darkness ahead of us. A crackling voice across the radio relays a message that catastrophic winds have ripped across Iowa and the reporters discuss a death march disguised as an election while the sky blinks in balmy storm lights against other kinds of veins. pink_sissy sips on stale coffee as she continues driving through the night, cuts off the news, rolls down the windows as the storm front mixes with the tears dripping off her cheeks, stares straight ahead as she reaches for my hand, holding it until we reach the dull haze of Saint Louis.

JULIAN TALAMANTEZ BROLASKI

my voice was too obvious

my voice was too obvious
an aunt gertrude or an uncle josh telling me
I'd never gosh or heck or darn gosh I'd never
anatomize the parts inside me
in fact the parts-inside-me-called
weren't parts   or they were caverns that ought to be caves
or something, stalagmites that ought to be stalactites
that writing feeling xum on me again
xum thru me
tulips drooped but one buttery one didnt
or was the whole thing a dream
a restaurant approximating a beach
whos floors were covered in sand
jellyfish undulate   what seemed
to be grinding on a bit of kelp we hoped
it was sexual for them both
peered at them afterward
after the ceviche that wasnt ceviche w/ its cubes of potato filler
tacos that werent tacos w/ their 2 shrimps and false casings
everything covered in first world problems wheat and dairy
when maasaw laid out all the gifts of the world
the hopi chose corn the apache chose game
and bahana the white man chose wheat cuz it was easiest to carry
jellyfish's arms were waving   we came up close I said

what is that a little string tying it to the kelp are they fake
AR asked yes yes the surferman said who'd never
been on a surfboard   nothing was not only not what
it seemed to be   it was not what it was   why bubble
the tank for a plastic fish   I must smoke
they say the seas are lousy w/ them   jellyfish
who can w/stand the acids + the poisons + the recordhigh
temperatures and decibels of the 7 plus wars we have going on
there like the bats they say at the museum of
jurassic technology that can fly thru concrete walls
they just slip thru the fishing nets easy as pie
down the throat of that fat kid in stand by me who
induces an entire midwestern town into a vomitorium
you can listen to the cry of this bat on a rotary phone mounted to the wall
easy as pie easy as fish easy as fishcake thru the cracks I cancelled
class to write this poem I a little bit counted chickens
mugwort thats for dreaming thats for later
eye twitched I had everything I had
'it all'   but if the pen were to fall
btwn the cracks of the firescape
if 'the grove divided into double parts'
and in I enterred was   or if I lissome
or proved to be the very mount I rode in on
'so mote it be'   actual sad cypress
ODB
what do you see
aside from what you see
power is in the periphery
or so I'm told
I want to smoke at my desk but I'm kind
I'm kind I am my kind   fat starling
sparrows fuss n fight but plesantly
what do these collocations hope for
babushka crumbs

vertical lines in negative as rays
merely the print of the bars
of a thing that never meant to be my jail
luminescing the underside of my eyes
record skip
along my mind
what do it I
what do it I
whuttdoitI
record do skip
along the needle of my mind

against breeding

for CAConrad

garbage-gut humans should not continue ourselves

it can only come a frightful cropper

hairbulbs what I mistook to be   a form in nature

albatross w/ plastics crowding thir gut

what julie patton is callin *superfraja-lilly-of-the-valley*

veronica heterophilia   snapdragon nature preserve

pulp them   shropshire constabulary

quing of haven   sailing for caracas   sissy jesus-hag

point to the exact place where the fly shd go in the ballo underpants

just where the shapes   come to a point triangularly

15 thousand fish dead at the mouth of tha mississipp

planes go sipsip   saying to the poor people

walk fa-ast!   walk like yr on hot co-als!

matisse had to get up real close   to see that was a burd

turned that viol de gamba right fwds   & added a noose

even more clîché than   peaches inna bowl

curvy long pear stem and   butterdish suspended

in air   perhaps the stem is penetrating a clear butter dish

conrad suggested   & I knew I was being drawn

into a funhouse of mirrors but I cdnt stop

odilon redon   roger & angelica

why I am against breeding

in the cut

for Cedar Sigo

"his being punished / for talking Indian."
—Cedar Sigo, "Prince Valiant"

person of clear salt water
warm clear deer

the mosquitoes I am
delicious to them
because of my fairy
or my indian blood

he is immune
to poison ivy
because indians dont
call it poison

utter unfaith in humanity
the leaves dont turn right
the leaves so that
they dont know how to turn right

when the guy at the bodega
complained about white ppl & gentrifications
you said me and my friend are native
I'm Suquamish, look it up

I vaporize the weed
we had for breakfast when
I come home from the poetry reading
thinking how low & how lively
we know of the cut

droppd my parasol in a ditch
pretend it didnt happen

on loneliness

"I have said that most patients keep their loneliness hidden as a secret from others, often even from themselves." —Freida Fromm-Reichmann, 'Loneliness' 16.

"horses chewing through the narrative." —erica lewis, *Darryl Hall is my Boyfriend*

when the rains finally came, they were relentless
the ground, unaccustomed to moisture
after years of drought, was forced to reject
the thing it craved the most
and floods peopled our every vein and the
cracked riverbed wept—its tears ran down—w/out feeling—
like whisky off a duck's back
truly complementary colors make a neutral
if I was made to remark
the polar vortex is strong in you
perhaps it wasn't so much
the oscillation in us
of some kind of arctic impulse
or oceanic feeling
toward what I perceive to be our relation
but rather, as always, it was my own
projection or transference or ocular
hallucination—which one can see is a pleasurable labor—
—silk pricked out with gold—
orange and blue is the exception—tho
they are complements, together they made a green, not muddy n/t
I was awake enough to be grossed out by your joke
but in a nice way, like a dog delights to tramp about in mud
Deborah says that Love entails the danger of destruction

whose heat humps thru the bedsheets
like a black hole bends the universe
or a mass is wracked along a frame
when the skunk sneaks in bed with the dog, ugh s(w)oon it has to hold
its nose, and eventually the violence, it flings the skunk
in disgust to the curb
funny, except the distress is authentic
say righteousness is an impulse toward being comely
just ask the one smurfette
how is she supposed to fend off all those smurves
or wtf cd a feminism even mean in that context
where everyone is blue
except gargamel and azrael, thinly veiled evil jew and cat antagonists
vocal fry making sad heron noises
headed to zorgonia off the x line in queens
profound experience of missing out
gillyham, arden, cokaygne, up to my neck in shit for seven years
the ramshackle succulents were about to bloom
we are engemmed in Victorian England
by virtue of Sherlock's mind palace
the horses
chewing thru the narration
were authentic, scooby doo was authentic, Lozen was authentic, its hearts
were haunted as in
a pavilion where you pay with meat
our gazes cross, unmet
D. says that loneliness is a disbelief
in the possibility of Love
I hid it so well
I hid it from myself
no ordinary sorrow
but—say righteousness is impassable on along a pollen path
a belief in being comely
a kodachrome you would take from me

along w/ the ill-fitting hats
and my belief in myself
as some kind of speculative cartography—
        composed of trees
                intermittent mountains
                        dope caballiers
—except the distress is authentic

KAMDEN HILLIARD

WELL ORGANIZED NOTE ON GOVERNANCE, OR, WAKE UP, SHEEPLE!

No1 will take me upon
proposal: a cosmic ant

hology of shame? "No," 4
ample legions. How we

mite dievest of the tailpipe's
chug-a gluging. Or, hors

d'oeuvres divorced from
order, dioxin. Or how

the box I out
think does not exist;

not unyielding nor un
yielding but rather is

an "opportunity zone,"
"development program,"

"grant." Or how it all goes
down like *gotcha* shit.

Proposal: nice sidewalks,
very wide. Level. No concrete,

maybe cork. Proposal : free
people forever. This

America *is* a solution as is
"round up," a solution,

as is orange –the agent—
orange –the color i love—

orange. What has been w
any application we might've

shared amicably? I am,
in part(s), mourning color. I

am, in parcels, tryna pass
on gratuitous hope.

The Tetsuo Harano Tunnels Are Colonial Infrastructure !

This road takes me home, this road is a bypass, & this road
is under construction . Thus , the lane ahead closes ; narrows
in 1 mouth & out the other .

The US military made it thru the mountain w blasting
bellies full of fluff piece & infrastructure
bc the US Military put their objects where your objects is.
bc the US Military say "good night" .
bc the US Military say wine is coffee-life & in-between the heart is a
lonely house hunter , where we settled on freezing all the head(s) .
Something about stock , but I've grown
sick from eating
            eating
            eating   thru the dead .

KASHIF
SHARMA-PATEL

ekphrastic motion

wu tsang
ekphrastic motion
that golden shimmer
in city farm allure
a rewind auratic
retention
in keeled knots
surface the indigent
a hanging parameter
revealed tactile
stained glass rays
in multi-formal
conviviality

acker fury
writing walls cut
down voice
cleared out faculty
fanciful forwardness
an imperial stance
senseless obdurate
set a — light

jay bernard

city mourning

gender cut embodied

tongue wrapped

mongrel assimilation

progressively becoming

counteractive — collapsing

we spoke in quick time

double step

deep routes

felt body licked

hidden in taste

the two genders (on mangoes and watermelons)

at the turn movement
too fast where undergirdings
switch locals affronted
as magazine shoots innocuous
glances in icy conditions
conditioning rays at the
corner of virtuous assembly
colonial marking in attire
subgenre dis-attachment
reverberates as legibility
cleans

shards of overground warmth
in midsts of atmospheric assault
furtive retreats into rhythms
foreknowing first
mangoes of the season
the originary tale of the cultivar
golden and alphonso judgements
crude shouts besmirching badamis
swelled noses and men in skull caps
wheeling juicy tales
compelling myths of origin
a kind of bare veniality

outpouring at another rotation
axial limits in guarded
contrapuntal melody

where the rain comes operation
voice regales, recounts,
earnest and weighty
continentality right

multiple dis-triangulations in
laughter
non-fluous
sweet surprises
in swift succinct strokes
at tip of watermelon knife
layering dreams past done

thresholds (after mahmoud darwish and bülent ersoy)

invisible visible
the making before birth
as threshold of identity
absent in its point
bodily transaction
presented in prehistoric
violence
along the stretch of contemporary
freedoms
voice transferred for bleeding
presents

if halfcut at axis when trauma turn left and coaches stand at operations in check, istanbul futures on bridging scars where wounds cauterise at the half-axial movement, modesty's mistress mistrust interpellative action ready-made already done in-action / daily humdrum urban milieu, sunflower pops, spread of salad, chorba and cacik, chai sipped in ancient action from saucer to tip, traumatic recurrences papered over with lino / rock psych and western garb / neo-europe as post-asia / polyglot returned as de-transitioned exchange / goods revealed orally, pre-auratic stance wrapped in plastic, paper-bag running cherry-tasting / vegan summoning in venture entrepreneurial ethno-business in linen-stripes and faulty light-switches

/ permeable archipelagic ardour as parabola pasts intersect at disjunctive points – cultural, epistemic, performative – turkic presents, london town fecundity in social breakdown – waking deaths – unmarked problems, urban problems – passive polities, politically rife, resolute insolence, antagonistic elevations – unsuccessful navigations in colony collapses, culinary conditions for ripening palates / aesthetic form distributed inordinate and detached / detailed debasements laundered in high-rise shores / widening paths occidentosis in post-islamicate tomfoolery / verlust at the hole-in-the-wall post-prole pre-capitalist perfidy / performed resignations / i breathe confessional warmth / i eat in essence / in pre-common state / i wish to bodily frame / through the blessed queers / the pre-lingual affectation, the movement of lingual judgement and nominative justice / the face of an-other / one an-other / browning health / sub-porous intent / an ethical recognition / the canteen as relation / the disinterested hospitality as being brought into the fold / choice done away with / bedecked in throes of wonder, guilt, fomo, restlessness looking to us here in content gliding possibility

/ after the event vibes

in wakening softening cherry skins,
taut (socratic) growing burdens of speech imposition –
outed inferences in the growing toil –
i was speaking rhetorically –
the conversation kept on non-verbal –
communication continue –
tanning slowly under kitsch suites –
dulling desires, caught in two –
over leisure in multiple desires tanning
consumerist in a bid for connection –
destructuring reminisces as post-nostalgic /
the conversing in absence after *absence* /
a further coming down /

evading a figures placed bodily straight and strict /
machine gun coloured administration in the head
weighing down like the original subalterns /
twisted queer lives – multivalent – street smart *girl* /
weathered woman, service male, petit flaneur,
casualised poet, pre-fabulatory gusto and angst

KAY GABRIEL

You Say Wife

Dear Kay—

A letter in seven arguments.

1. ON LIES

In another poem a man compares me to pussy, and then it happens again. Rosario says straight men don't even *like* pussy, an attack so devastating I took it vicariously. Cause of death: personal correspondence. Do I care about straight men? The question is maybe misplaced.

Anyways they care about me. That coy interval between gays and trans women is good for a couple things, one of which is giving the lie to hetero protestations about themselves. I don't even believe them, culprits of their own desire, though as Cam says I think they believe themselves.

This thing is multiform, contingent, ambivalent and I call her my sex. Even if I make choices I still like everything. I like myself and you, but the hole we share accuses us both. I'll call it autofiction; on its head it accuses the world.

2. ON HIGH SCHOOL

VISITING HOURS ARE OVER FOR THE BLOODBATH, PLEASE

3. ON BEING A WIFE

Q: Are you polymorphously perverse?
A: No, I am betrothed to the present.

Consider the wife. Desperately Seeking Susan: Rosanna Arquette, wed to a jacuzzi and skimming the personals, rearranges the opposite side of the bridge. Anybody can be Madonna, so everybody's a wife in Fort Lee. Even the tubs dull the senses into a staycation. Arquette wants to be a club kid too, and briefly succeeds—at the precinct, in a gutted loft. Get into the groove and rot there, oh comely *bohèmes*! You'll even like it.

You say wife like style or you say wife like rifled through someone else's stocks or you say wife like wages. Wearing only animal print and plump in the right places. Dear Kay. Suspicious, you delayed wifery. Now you wear it like a polymer mink. Anybody can be a wife in the country like everybody's a piece in town.

Q: Does everybody feel this way?
A: I suspect they do, the fuckers

4. ON JOIE DE VIVRE

It comes out of me like *ohhhhhhhh*

5. ON BEAUTY

"By origin or not I am 'of' the city until I can't be—a choice, as choices go, made within constraints, one of which is surely beauty." I'm saying beauty like a person, not aesthetics like a grad student, though for my sins I'm the persona of a grad student and I've been one for long enough it feels like a condition.

You say aesthetics like style or you say aesthetics like a pretty face or you say aesthetics like a brand. Brecht says you can't write poems about trees when the woods are full of cops. An aesthete says you can't write poems about sex if the city's full of brands. Or: art has no vocation after 1991. Or: beauty is a fixing for the wealthy, a commons in a paywall. Do I like this world and what it's full of? Like hell but there it goes, spitting you in the face and waiting for you underwater. You don't refuse to breathe, do you?

Meanwhile behind this handwringing the hushed suggestion that women, gays, transsexuals are especially to blame for the miseries of brands, or what the metropole inflicts on everybody else. Hello, I hate it. Or: how interesting, the smack of the feminized in buying and selling.

Dear Kay, hi, I'm waging a sub rosa war. Who loves me will know what I mean.

6. ON GRIEF

It comes out of me like god fucking damnit......

7. ON LIES

Desire is the *suture* of a *new* (say it) world—*I'll fuck you till your dick is blue*—following Jackie's lead it won't be one of winners in a virtuous game, or letting agency skid off your ethical shoulders, or of sharing your toys based on a common Rx.

What are you and what does it mean for me a question nobody could stop asking if they wanted. *Re: perversion* you meant to say and follow it with something about *bodying forth the new* but Rachel heard one word played together like a chord. Say it's the same old sex bent double. It's mine now, and goes between me like a stent.

Dear Kay. I'm writing the same letter always, let me try it again. Here's a fable in the perfect tense: some friends—perpetually adolescent and vengeful, with a weekend off and no particular reputation—make the drive to bully a medium-famous writer. He's speaking at a private college for a couple hundred bucks a pop, the subject "modernist difficulty" or you get the idea. They've got a megaphone, which they use to frighten local wildlife. The poets they intended to swirlie have all scattered to satisfy their appetites on bowls of seasonal produce. Or maybe the Rimbaldian creatures enjoy their promised encounter after all, irritate the Tenure out of every mom and dad. Campus cops usher them off the handsome private greens. Over fries the *maudit* kids hum some poems about difficulty, poetry and rent, which makes them feel a little better—even triumphant!

Two of them are dating, and sort of clocky. En route back to a dingy apartment in the 'burbs some guy on the train resents the way their faces look, how they touch each other. He's got a couple slurs to share—his parting shot to "stay away from that AIDS." Which missile, however graphic, lets something slip.

I'd like to say that he got his but actually he disembarked at Newark without consequences. It's a shame for words to be more vibrant than sex—and sexier, too, says my enthusiastic boyfriend. Write back with something genuinely new, I won't be disconsolate or have anything unkind to say, palpating that world in a caress, your palpatrix on call,

Turner

I Could Go On

Dear Jo:

Good morning, I'm shallow, sleepless, irrepressible. Does that endear me to you? 5 AM in March, wind smacks the skylight and hustles refuse over Flatbush like somebody's idea of a Zeitgeist. *Hi* it says *time to nap* but instead I'm writing testaments of what and who I love—Mike is sleeping in my bed warm and furred like a cat with a beard and a tattoo sleeve, maybe he would resent that description, I can do no other, I'm awake in another room achieving nothing in the second person singular, hello.

I do it for God and the television, with a promiscuous heart. I do it with prosthetics but à propos of anybody with an opinion about them: you are *forbidden* I want to say from evaluating my *component parts*, I am an atom, fuck a metonymy, fuck a catalogue. First I composed that sentence, then I felt myself get eyebanged by every guy with a beard on the subway platform, don't think, Jo, I didn't sometimes return the favour. Mike's gone now, who brought me Oreos and spooned while I dreamt my nipples turned into mice and died, it's spring and I've been eyeing every aging wonder boy in the park plus his leanly pumping quads, their sprigs of magnificent hair, there's even crocuses, furious purple delicate violet contemptuous yellow, now I'm on a train, hello.

My imaginative lusts riddle bullet holes in the side of *the achievable*. Have you ever wanted to get fucked by an abdomen, an armpit, a couple of peddling legs? My preferred position with Cam for instance letting him piledrive my face from above, I lie down on my bed like a failed porn actor, I can imagine the camera fixed on my dewy lined eyes the bottom half of my face obscured under a cock and a tremendous cupid's bow my cheeks sharp enough to be an architectural instrument as both of us try to remember our lines—but from this POV it's more like sex with a wiry frame and faded punk tattoos. Halfway into Jersey anyways and I'm I thinking about your letter, poem, whatever, "All I Want by Joni Mitchell," where every paragraph begins *I want*. *I* is the letter's only person, *want* its only verb. It's Monday morning, what do I want? The flourishing of bees and grasses, never for anyone to pay rent, for the landlord to stop, for fuck's sake, *spying* on us, also a backyard, to speak veritably about no appetite, never again authenticated, no more bad-faith prurience no more AWP, my done taxes, a living wage for CUNY adjuncts, no moving apartments no falling to pieces, various men, if only they could finger, only some items impossible some are consequential, I fill up the tank and say goodnight and go, I could go on.

Patty Schemel writes in her memoir she joined Hole after "Doll Parts" was already cut but wrote a new drum line for the end and can still hear the more ambitious resonance of her snare in the final 16 bars or so sounding a hollow trench for Courtney's appetite *I fake it so real* I regularly dream I'm in a band but of course can play no instrument instead I writhe on stage exacerbating attention my face flushing well really my ears and my own desperate hot need to be seen, dear Jo, you get me.

So what if I want to be embarrassed? Usually I feel like telling anybody your dreams feels like showing your ass to strangers, well, so what if they look at what's good for them. Last night dreamt of being flat, ran all night to the top of my own dimension, night before the dream about the mice, then I came into possession of an immense stash, pursued by dream police I hid my ketamine in the pastel candy shop of other pharmaceuticals—even in dreams I can purloin a letter!—but the cops in my head got wise to the trick, even to a daring cinematic escape down a garbage chute where a "man with facial hair tries to recall my identity." By train through Jersey no spring here yet everything brown enclosed backyarded, and what have they done with my full stops, the Wawa in reach, I'm Dunkin, I'm somebody's sugary kid.

Call embarrassment less a discomfiting bug and more an intransigent object of megafixation, a hot flash an indisputable even if unconfirmed certainty of *occupying somebody's attention despite themselves* whether in vexation mockery or aimless arousal though maybe now my sense of shame a fruit rotted on the vine   like for instance to trick myself back to sleep watch videos of anybody else eating things I can't or won't like soups and noodles, foods on a stick, McDonalds breakfasts, lunch meats, eggs fried into toast oh hell   as in a *letter from* or *season in*   a staycation in hell Good hell morning I haven't slept again I think I'm amorous infrastructure

Jo I think you're a lyricist of infatuation and I'm a geographer of arousal. What, if any, is the relevant difference, how will we be graded, I'm a slice of cake and cream, I'm Michelle Trachtenberg in *Mysterious Skin* and you're my malfortunate Joseph Gordon Levitt, we applaud each others' poor decisions, late for work again goodnight you run up my phone bill I lie for hours in the hot water we toast with our remaining vices and make up about it, mutual spectators in the tragedy of semi-notorious men. Does that endear me to you? We're on the run from one to another parking lot, one of us a cavalier drifter with life by the balls, the other a neurotic but the better driver, with hair "the colour of eyeliner" which am I? You're a caramelized peach, poached, juiced, even at a distance so inconvenient it'd take a day to reach you by bus on several tumescent roads.

Can you hear me where you sleep? Dear Jo. I want to fingerfuck my boyfriend in this bar, and I want you to know I'm thinking about it. Surprise!

With love at a boil,
Turner

LAUREL UZIELL

from T

1.

Captive in semblance: the body cam protruding inwards, there is the image of a shattered contradiction cuts the lungflesh just across its edge. Bleed out, the trace of all inside now public, but it always was. To make the shocks more smooth, less ruptural, the same way that an enemy is made to nature. The law attempts to describe its object even as it makes it, now everyone must either be the perpetrator or the victim of a hate crime. Things change: this is simultaneously true and violently unutterable, grammar with a broken neck, one's migration into many at any level, still spliced, still whole.

4.

A particular quantity of wrong discards
it's quality, or maybe not, statistically im-
poverished for care of me. What you
could call abstraction has always been
the ground we stood on as well as just its
order. Dis-
position to the wind, triggered mutant pre-
fix, the vast immutable economy of organs
suffix to the real world swallowed outward,
raw material and processed food. 'It is
human nature to stand in the middle of a
thing'. The
middle shrunken to a rotten disc, crudely
empirical, as custom or compulsion to re-
peat. What does this have to do with how
we live our lives, unvoiced beneath the
clotted sky, the chaotic silence of natural
law. In-
herent flaw repeated. The hole is a window
through which you speak, for what becomes
a norm, just how much can you bear.

LESLIE FEINBERG

from Stone Butch Blues

DEAR THERESA,

I'm lying on my bed tonight missing you, my eyes all swollen, hot tears running down my face. There's a fierce summer lightning storm raging outside. Tonight I walked down streets looking for you in every woman's face, as I have each night of this lonely exile. I'm afraid I'll never see your laughing, teasing eyes again.

I had coffee in Greenwich Village earlier with a woman. A mutual friend fixed us up, sure we'd have a lot in common since we're both "into politics." Well, we sat in a coffee shop and she talked about Democratic politics and seminars and photography and problems with her co-op and how she's so opposed to rent control. Small wonder—Daddy is a real estate developer.

I was looking at her while she was talking, thinking to myself that I'm a stranger in this woman's eyes. She's looking at me but doesn't see me. The she finally said how she hates this society for what it's done to "women like me" who hate themselves so much they have to look and act like men. I felt myself getting flushed and my face twitched a little and I started telling her, all cool and calm, about how women like me existed since the dawn of time, before there was oppression, and how those societies respected them, and she got her very interested expression on—and besides it was time to leave.

So we walked by a corner where these cops were laying into a homeless man and I stopped and mouthed off to the cops and they started coming at me with their clubs raised and she tugged my belt to pull me back. I just looked at her, and suddenly I felt things well up in me I thought I had buried. I stood there remembering you like I didn't see cops about to hit me, like I was falling back into another world, a place I wanted to go again.

And suddenly my heart hurt so bad and I realized how long it's been since my heart felt—anything.

I need to go home to you tonight, Theresa. I can't. So I'm writing you this letter.

I remember years ago, the day I started working at the cannery in Buffalo and you had already been there a few months, and how your eyes caught mine and played with me before you set me free. I was supposed to be following the foreman to fill out some forms but I was so busy wondering what color your hair was under that white paper net and how it would look and feel in my fingers, down loose and free. And I remember how you laughed gently when the foreman came back and said, "You comin' or not?"

All of us he-shes were mad as hell when we heard you got fired because you wouldn't let the superintendence touch your breasts. I still unloaded on the docks for another couple of days, but I was kind of mopey. It just wasn't the same after your light went out.

I couldn't believe it the night I went to the club on the West Side. There you were, leaning up against the bar, your jeans too tight for words and your hair, your hair all loose and free.

And I remember that look in your eyes again. You didn't just know me, you liked what you saw. And this time, ooh woman, we were on our own turf. I could move the way you wanted me to, and I was glad I'd gotten all dressed up.

Our own turf . . . "Would you dance with me?"

You didn't say yes or no, just teased me with your eyes, straightened my tie, smoothed my collar, and took me by the hand. You had my heart before you moved against me like you did. Tammy was singing "Stand By Your Man," and we were changing all the he's to she's inside our heads to make it fit right. After you moved that way, you had more than my heart. You made me ache and you liked that. So did I.

The older butches warned me: if you wanted to keep your marriage, don't go to the bars. But I've always been a one-woman butch. Besides, this was our community, the only one we belonged to, so we went every weekend.

There were two kinds of fights in the bars. Most weekends had one kind or the other, some weekends both. There were the fist fights between butch women—full of booze, shame, jealous insecurity. Sometimes the fights were awful and spread like a web to trap everyone in the bar, like the night Heddy lost her eye when she got hit upside the head with a bar stool.

I was real proud that in all those years I never hit another butch woman. See, I loved them too, and I understood their pain and their shame because I was so much like them. I loved the lines etched in their faces and hands and the curves of their work- weary shoulders. Sometimes I looked in the mirror and wondered what I would look like when I was their age. Now I know!

In their own way, they loved me too. They protected me because they knew I wasn't a "Saturday-night butch." The weekend butches were scared of me because I was a stone he-she.

If only they had known how powerless I really felt inside! But the older butches, they knew the whole road that lay ahead of me and they wished I didn't have to go down it because it hurt so much.

When I came into the bar in drag, kind of hunched over, they told me, "Be proud of what you are," and then they adjusted my tie sort of like you did. I was like them; they knew I didn't have a choice. So I never fought them with my fists. We clapped each other on the back in the bars and watched each other's backs at the factory.

But then there were the times our real enemies came in the front door : drunken gangs of sailors, Klan-type thugs, sociopaths and cops. You always knew when they walked in because someone thought to pull the plug on the jukebox. No matter how many times it happened, we all still went "Aw . . . " when the music stopped and then realized it was time to get down to business. When the bigots came in, it was time to fight, and fight we did. Fought hard—femme and butch, women and men together.

If the music stopped and it was the cops at the door, someone plugged the music back in and we switched dance partners. Us in our suits and ties paired off with our drag queen sisters in their dresses and pumps. Hard to remember that it was illegal then for two women or two men to sway to music together. When the music ended, the butches bowed, our femme partners curtsied, and we returned to our seats, our lovers, and our drinks to await our fates.

That's when I remember your hand on my belt, up under my suit jacket. That's where your hand stayed the whole time the cops were there. "Take it easy, honey. Stay with me baby, cool off," you'd be cooing in my ear like a special lover's song sung to warriors who need to pick and choose their battles in order to survive.

We learned fast that the cops always pulled the police van right up to the bar door and left snarling dogs inside so we couldn't get out. We were trapped, alright.

Remember the night you stayed home with me when I was so sick? That was the night—you remember. The cops picked out the most stone butch of them all to destroy with humiliation, a woman everyone said "wore a raincoat in the shower." We heard they stripped her, slow, in front of everyone in the bar, and laughed at her trying to cover up her nakedness. Later she went mad, they said. Later she hung herself.

What would I have done if I had been there that night? I'm remembering the busts in the bars in Canada. Packed in the police vans, all the Saturday-night butches giggled and tried to fluff up their hair and switch clothing so they could get thrown in the tank with the femme women—said it would be like "dyin' and goin' to heaven." The law said we had to be wearing three pieces of women's clothing.

We never switched clothing. Neither did our drag queen sisters. We knew, and so did you, what was coming. We needed our sleeves rolled up, our hair slicked back, in order to live through it. Our hands were cuffed tight behind our backs. Yours were cuffed in front. You loosened my tie, unbuttoned my collar, and touched my face. I saw the pain and fear for me in your face, and I whispered it would be alright. We knew it wouldn't be.

I never told you what they did to us down there—queens in one tank, stone butches in the next—but you knew. One at a time they would drag our brothers out of the cells, slapping and punching them, locking the bars behind them fast in case we lost control and tried to stop them, as if we could. They'd handcuff a brother's wrists to his ankles or chain his face against the bars. They made us watch. Sometimes we'd catch the eyes of the terrorized victim, or the soon-to-be, caught in the vise of torture, and we'd say gently, "I'm with you, honey, look at me, it's OK, we'll take you home."

We never cried in front of the cops. We knew we were next. The next time the cell door opens it will be me they drag out and chain spread-eagle to the bars.

Did I survive? I guess I did. But only because I knew I might get home to you.

They let us out last, one at a time, on Monday morning. No charges. Too late to call in sick to work, no money, hitch- hiking, crossing the border on foot, rumpled clothes, bloody, needing a shower, hurt, scared.

I knew you'd be home if I could get there.

You ran a bath for me with sweet-smelling bubbles. You laid out a fresh pair of white BVDs and a T-shirt for me and left me alone to wash off the first layer of shame.

I remember, it was always the same. I would put on the briefs, and then I'd just get the T-shirt over my head and you would find some reason to come into the bathroom, to get something or put something away. In a glance you would memorize the wounds on my body like a road map—the gashes, bruises, cigarette burns.

Later, in bed, you held me gently, caressing me everywhere, the tenderest touches reserved for the places I was hurt, knowing each and every sore place—inside and out. You didn't flirt with me right away, knowing I wasn't confident enough to feel sexy. But slowly you coaxed my pride back out again by showing me how much you wanted me. You knew it would take you weeks again to melt the stone.

Lately I've read these stories by women who are so angry with stone lovers, even mocking their passion when they finally give way to trust, to being touched. And I'm wondering: did it hurt you the times I couldn't let you touch me? I hope it didn't. You never showed it if it did. I think you knew it wasn't you I was keeping myself safe from. You treated my stone self as a wound that needed loving healing. Thank you. No one's ever done that since. If you were here tonight ... well, it's hypothetical, isn't it?

I never said these things to you.

Tonight I remember the time I got busted alone, on strange turf. You're probably wincing already, but I have to say this to you. It was the night we drove ninety miles to a bar to meet friends who never showed up. When the police raided the club we were "alone," and the cop with gold bars on his uniform came right over to me and told me to stand up. No wonder, I was the only he-she in the place that night.

He put his hands all over me, pulled up the band of my Jockeys and told his men to cuff me—I didn't have three pieces of women's clothing on. I wanted to fight right then and there because I knew the chance would be lost in a moment.

But I also knew that everyone would be beaten that night if I fought back, so I just stood there. I saw they had pinned your arms behind your back and cuffed your hands. One cop had his arm across your throat. I remember the look in your eyes. It hurts me even now.

They cuffed my hands so tight behind my back I almost cried out. Then the cop unzipped his pants real slow, with a smirk on his face, and ordered me down on my knees. First I thought to myself, I can't! Then I said out loud to myself and to you and to him, "I won't!" I never told you this before, but something changed inside of me at that moment. I learned the difference between what I can't do and what I refuse to do.

I paid the price for that lesson. Do I have to tell you every detail? Of course not.

When I got out of the tank the next morning you were there. You bailed me out. No charges, they just kept your money. You had waited all night long in that police station. Only I knew how hard it was for you to withstand their leers, their taunts, their threats. I knew you cringed with every sound you strained to hear from back in the cells. You prayed you wouldn't hear me scream.

I didn't.

I remember when we got outside to the parking lot you stopped and put your hands lightly on my shoulders and avoided my eyes. You gently rubbed the bloody places on my shirt and said, "I'll never get these stains out."

Damn anyone who thinks that means you were relegated in life to worrying about my ring-around-the-collar.

I knew exactly what you meant. It was such an oddly sweet way of saying, or not saying, what you were feeling. Sort of the way I shut down emotionally when I feel scared and hurt and helpless and say funny little things that seem so out of context.

You drove us home with my head in your lap all the way, stroking my face. You ran the bath. Set out my fresh underwear. Put me to bed. Caressed me carefully. Held me gently.

Later that night I woke up and found myself alone in bed. You were drinking at the kitchen table, head in your hands. You were crying. I took you firmly in my arms and held you, and you struggled and bit my chest with your fists because the enemy wasn't there to fight. Moments later you recalled the bruises on my chest and cried even harder, sobbing, "It's my fault, I couldn't stop them."

I've always wanted to tell you this. In that one moment I knew you really did understand how I felt in life. Choking on anger, feeling so powerless, unable to protect myself or those I loved most, yet fighting back again and again, unwilling to give up. I didn't have the words to tell you this then. I just said, "It'll be OK, it'll be alright." And then we smiled ironically at what I'd said, and I took you back to our bed and made the best love to you I could, considering the shape I was in. You knew not to try to touch me that night. You just ran your fingers through my hair and cried and cried.

When did we get separated in life, sweet warrior woman? We thought we'd won the war of liberation when we embraced the word gay. Then suddenly there were professors and doctors and lawyers coming out of the woodwork telling us that meetings should be run with Robert's Rules of Order. (Who died and left Robert god?)

They drove us out, made us feel ashamed of how we looked. They said we were male chauvinist pigs, the enemy. It was women's hearts they broke. We were not hard to send away, we went quietly.

The plants closed. Something we never could have imagined. That's when I began passing as a man. Strange to be exiled from your own sex to borders that will never be home.

You were banished too, to another land with your own sex, and yet forcibly apart from the women you loved as much as you tried to love yourself.

For more than twenty years I have lived on this lonely shore, wondering what became of you. Did you wash off your Saturday night makeup in shame? Did you burn in anger when women said, "If I wanted a man I'd be with a real one?"

Are you turning tricks today? Are you waiting tables or learning Word Perfect 5.1?

Are you in a lesbian bar looking out of the corner of your eye for the butchest woman in the room? Do the women there talk about Democratic politics and seminars and co-ops? Are you with women who only bleed monthly on their cycles?

Or are you married in another blue-collar town, lying with an unemployed auto worker who is much more like me than they are, listening for the even breathing of your sleeping children? Do you bind his emotional wounds the way you tried to heal mine?

Do you ever think of me in the cool night?

I've been writing this letter to you for hours. My ribs hurt bad from a recent beating. You know.

I never could have survived this long if I'd never known your love. Yet still I ache with missing you and need you so.

Only you could melt this stone. Are you ever coming back?

The storm has passed now. There is a pink glow of light on the horizon outside my window. I am remembering the nights I fucked you deep and slow until the sky was just this color.

I can't think about you anymore, the pain is swallowing me up. I have to put your memory away, like a precious sepia photograph. There are still so many things I want to tell you, to share with you.

Since I can't mail you this letter, I'll send it to a place where they keep women's memories safe. Maybe someday, passing through this big city, you will stop and read it. Maybe you won't.

Good night, my love.

LEVI BENTLEY

slender oat rehearse*

claudia and hen
show up in language
see
here they are
how does one show up to the world?
precipitating into it?
claudia and hen float up
an avalanche of bottles hits
the dumpster outside the bar

outside my bedroom sometime
after two am
trying to reach hen and claudia again
thinking this rewrites it
claudia laughing puts a hand on hen's shoulder
there is something easy about it and an ache
about how one does how does one go about waking
into a filigree of limbs sometimes
my own
it seems
to keep happening but now

* title taken from a translation of Virgil's Eclogues.

i've lost them again claudia and hen

are digging up

the street in front of the house

they've put a fence up a line

of social text that keeps in capital, keeps out need

see, around the vegetable garden there

is a hole at the center

of the garden as deep as a grave

i resurface through

a chemical blue of sleep again

showing up pressed against glass points visible

through a chemical

blue

an over-the-counter blue

sometimes one is an unreadable point and no kind of

future is legible

against the window of the eight ball of the world

the body floats up from sleep words come down

they are heavy they fall

into sentences

what are you willing

to *sentence* here?

it has to be done carefully; the breaking

and entering

a kind of guerilla gardening i fall in and out of love with

language

claudia and hen get on with life

they watch me from their careful fence

safe behind nominal boundary, an iron script

how do you decide what shows up here?

claudia and hen don't need it

they offer tea insincerely they suggest it is time to leave

i am falling through *language* to get to you
        feeling through the dark of *language*
        at the edge of sleep just surfacing
i am waiting at the clean edge of silence for something
        i wake up again and again tangled and stung
        a body, pricked with itching shadowed by pain
                                there is *something*
there
i came here because i did not know how to write a love letter
    i still do not
        all the language i have is proprietary
            it all wraps back into the same bad thing
the available parts
    however assembled
        build the same machine
claudia and hen have finished their doomsday device
    there it is inside a door at the bottom of the grave-sized
hole
        inside their garden
i can't get the dream back
    where they weren't yet building

LIAM O'BRIEN

Set you down first:
acres of frost
then: *acres of thaw*

then: *both of us*
live under law.

You came up in a green land
shoulders high
over the sea.

I had some green men
to crow over me.

We will set it down
and make bread
and pay the rent:

neither one of us
will be president.

It Is Not Safe

fragments from *The Complete Home*, Julia McNair Wright, 18-25

In this home their occupations are all the inventions
of the world's animate heart. Erase all homes, all home life,
ties, needs, and joys—would the wheels of labor move?

Man without object is Home. Tremendous cost. What have you,
in yourself? A root of feeling? Count the cost. Mercy.
I should be frightened. The first thing needful.

I do not believe there are principles not established
on the heart. So strong, the onset of the world.
Flesh and the devil on shifting sands. Decisions I refuse.

The foundation of a home: I should have thought love.
Left out. Love that will not grow weary. Love that has
a night-shade, leaving nature. Marrying the world,

in loyal love, a corner-stone. Have you that love? Low
love? Only a heart, I have lived. *What will become
of me?* Love so enduring must be thorough. The intimacy

between, changing unlikeness—that manner of engagement.
Not so fast, my dear. I should want time enough to lay,
to grow, to give love a shock. It will endure. *I am afraid.*

My beloved, change your law. No wonder love shows itself.
To build up a corner-stone. Courage to lay down circumstance.
To care for the last, the life-misery. A young man to accept

his disasters. Men marry, and men. A man finds the struggle
how much harder? As healthful and happy as others.
But some disease, which speedily developed, keeps longer.

Lesser than friendships, God, and humanity. Long-enduring,
prepared to meet. That Home, build up within. A man
has nothing: he has no right to be. There should be something.

Burdened, to increase and not diminish:
nothing so breaks. Let every man take.
It is not safe: to love one another.

LISTEN CHEN

like the moon when freed from the clouds

a slender midsection of the clock behind the guard's station being visible from the small window in cell 1 a prisoner may peer out & confirm whether it is or is not 12 o'clock or 6 o'clock or on the hour or half past something providing

a guard does not shutter the view *Let him not despise*

what he has received the strains of personhood cradled by a stiff white blanket a thin mat a stainless steel ligature-resistant toilet a name carved into the door canned spaghetti toast powdered orange drink a styrofoam plate & cup one layer of the prisoner's own clothing & most humanely—if you know to ask—

a worn john grisham novel *O Bhikshu*

empty this boat! beneath the long arc of silence she assembles herself alone her disordered thoughts interrupted only by bootsteps keys jangling the unconcerned laughter of a guard or a metal door sliding open & then shut *good*

is restraint

in the ear without time & its corruscating ooze of contact & dependence only the vital no-self watches on w/ utmost indifference while seen or unseen

countless dead friends are treading calmly through the glittering mists of history *let him be perfect in his duties & in the fulness of delight he will make an end of*

suffering as the wind's intricate emptiness sweeps away the faces of pigs & sledge-
hammers leap out of bricks & the social shadow explodes from behind every
judge's *you* as *music alone awakens in man*

a sense of music jail awakens the mirage of not-jail that narrow bridge towering
over a world without possible escape like a fistful of sand

waiting to be scattered in the wind *A Bhikshu who delights in earnestness who looks with fear on thoughtlessness moves about like fire*

burning all his fetters small or large

this body is like froth

Once you've shaken them out of the can and swirled them around a bit

the ravioli do have the same basic shape Bullet Resistant Hollow Metal door and frame assemblies

are designed of "non-ricochet type" as depicted on the wrapper intended to permit capture and retention of attacking projectile lessening potential of random injury and the sauce is almost the right color

However the meat inside is not a healthy brown but rather a sickly gray

lateral penetration uses cold rolled steel prime painted steel

which is cut then broken and welded to size Frames includes armor

2" face to meet ballistic protection level The pasta too

is miscolored more a pasty white than a golden yellow Additionally the sauce doesn't coat the ravioli

like it's supposed to and the pasta pieces are more like flared-out boxes of meat with ballistic armor and foam insulation inserted to meet ballistic protection level

than fluffy little beef pillows The sauce required Assembly leaves factory swinging on frame

is really the only thing with a flavor so it's a good thing it's decent for having come out of a can that may have been on

the shelf for heavy duty clear anodized years The "pasta" is so soft

aluminum continuous gear hinge

that you can chew the whole meal prepped for cylinder mortise

with just your tongue

lockset exit device or the roof

of your mouth

弃智遗身

in the struggle for truth a person may disappear

all distances collapsed to the span of a few paces the inexhaustible walls clearing a path upon which to discard wisdom

& set the beloved body aside *what else*

need I ask from another the ecstatic hallucinations of death summoning forth a bedsheet a shoelace a plastic bag a light fixture a vent a window bar or an electrical cord that asks *twenty years or twenty minutes* to which the enlightened sees only *A shooting star a clouding of the sight a lamp An illusion a drop of dew a bubble A dream a lightning's*

flash a thunder cloud a flare longing to dissolve back into the smooth darkness of the night sky or a faded memory

of the night sky *Subhuti* ,

if bodhisattvas abide in the notions of a self a person a sentient being or a life span they are not

bodhisattvas after roughing in as required place fixture

in position and use as template to locate and mark flange points on floor where does a turnkey hide his human hands? the body draped against the cell puncturing the sunlit kitchen the quiet sunday the blue canadian expanse *If I had a job I would not commit crime If I had been arrested I would say I was sorry*

If I had a supportive family I would not kill myself I always turn up in court where the course of self-estrangement transcends self-estrangement *she mounted this pile of firewood and kindled a fire* their souls ascending in columns of smoke that mottle the civil sky *Within these walls I bid farewell*

to a strong calm bandit who had never killed while mantles of ash float along the sills of our ghostly dependence the myth of permanence

stumbling beneath looming walls crooked shadows turnkeys & getaways

LOGAN FEBRUARY

desire is poured upon your lovely face Aphrodite has honored you exceedingly

—Sappho, Fragment 112, trans. Anne Carson

staring at beautiful men   will get me killed someday
let it be a good glossy death   over the phone   I talk my shit
as the moon sinks into its own velvet   his bliss in my ear
like a cherry blossom   in real life   I'm gangly
I'm graceless   Boy Long Legs   I am asked to be insecure
and not know I'm alive   but here's sustained eye-contact
for you   I reopen my petals
at least remember   their tender hue
neglected   the violets will not survive the night
is this what fear   tastes like   this acid metal
legs won't go where eyes go   I said   carefree and not
death wish   the blade gleams that we live so close to
I must obey   here life is short even though everyone says
life is short   today I feel I am holding onto warm water
and falling

The Tidy Crimes of Personhood

How to be gratified and carry on in this life
Where no one gets what they want

I want to die
Happy after eating a giant bowl of spaghetti I want
So much water but only have these two beers
At 1pm I recalled the SOPHIE song I was going
To tell you about at 1am I thrashed my head against
The pillow in an attempt to shake out its tight melody
I blame so many things on the Buddhist in me

So many
Tidy crimes of personhood like I never returned your calls
After our tryst in the penthouse suite last November
Like I have never written a kind poem about my mother
Like once in secret I tried on a white dress and swooned
From the innocence in the mirror yes

Yes I would like
To upgrade my unfortunate body to become someone more
Like a goddess but kinder a little less eternal I would
Like to say very boastfully that I have detached myself
From all worldly things but that would not be true
I still love the slow burn of a shared joint spicy chicken
The savage gyrations of sex and I still hate liars

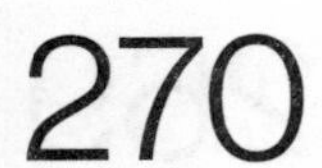

Men

Who make a hobby out of blood

I want to have my fingers in my ears saying

I cannot hear the noises of this world! but now again

The little voice is asking me if it is cold in the water

Yes

Yes it is quite cold

Girl of The Year

for E

I am outside of the filthy 21st century
I am in prehistoric Africa with my feet

Unbound and soaking in salt streams
I dream of a sky, having no word for its color

Having no murmurs and no worries
Everybody with problems of their own

I wear my costly beads, I wear my lace
I veil my face out of existence

My fate is to be well taken care of
To be polished with oil, with shea butter

To be a seam between nations at war
I have a wealth of headaches, of anger

Like a madwoman, I nurse
My eternal rage for which I have no name

Vowing to be nobody's bride
Unless he places his crown on my hair

LOU SULLIVAN

edited by Ellis Martin
and Zach Ozma

from We Both Laughed in Pleasure: The Selected Diaries of Lou Sullivan

My God, when he stands so near to me I feel like I'm going to be burned if he brushes against me. I can hardly hold myself back from taking hold of him. He looks like he tastes good. He smells good.

I said I was very complimented he came over. He said he's real lonely lately. I debated with myself whether to give him [Swinburne's] "Fragoletta," but decided against it at this time—no need to rush anything—we're having a 4th of July cook-out on the roof. I just told him I got into a real poetry-reading mood after everyone left from the party.

We drank tea + talked. He sees me watching him + pretends he doesn't + then he decides to give in + looks me right in the eye + laughs.

Why is he always teasing me?

Will I ever be able to kiss him. I wonder if this is all fantasy-land, or after some point he'll actually let me give him some of these physical pleasures he's craving so bad but wants from a true blue female. Ah, those 20-year-old hormones!

"Fragoletta" too gushing, too physical. I found instead "A Leave-Taking" by Swinburne.

So I did it. I gave him the poem. He immediately opened it in front of everyone + asked me, "What does this mean for you?" I answered, "It's a love poem."

He began reading it + asked what it meant. I said "It says it all there, better than I could say it." He said, "Then you're putting yourself down." I said don't read it here! He said, "I want to talk with you about this at your place." I was so shocked and nervous, I said, "What?" He repeated it.

COME HENCE
LET BE
LIE STILL; IT IS ENOUGH

He asked who wrote it, I said a turn-of-the-century English poet. Suddenly we were alone in the room + I said what did you want to talk about? He's sitting in an easy chair. I'm standing. He says, "What do you feel—inside—for me?" I answered, "I think I love you." He asked "Why?" I thought a second, recovering from his question—so blatant, so cutting, so disbelieving: I said, "Because I think about you a lot during the day." A smile came over his lips, he smiled at me + said "That's nice. Thank you."

I suggested we all go to a movie + he wanted to go get a sweater, I guess, so was going to meet us at the theatre. I asked, "Can I come with you, T?" He called back, "Sure Lou. If you want to." We went to his beautiful beautiful place. It was like Albion, but more beautiful. He said he built all the wood himself—a loft where he slept. I was enthralled. Mystified. He lived there 3 years with a 30-year-old roommate.

Suddenly we were sitting on the floor talking about some shit + we lost track of the conversation + I was gazing into his face + he asked, "What are you thinking about—RIGHT NOW." I started laughing, fell back on my elbows + answered, "I was thinking about how beautiful you are." He told me tht from the start he felt something special between us, too, and that he liked me a lot and thought we really had something good between us. That he really felt good that I told him how I felt. He said he didn't want to get into anything sexual with me, though, and I said, "Neither do I. That's what the poem says."

We ran together to the movie. I didn't arrange to sit next to him, but there he sat, next to me.

IF I FOLLOW MY HEART
I'M GONNA LOVE YOU

He fuckin let me kiss him in front of a big group of people, including Cuca. I said, "Look at this guy—he's an insatiable flirt. Have you no shame?—He has no shame, and I have no scruples."

He told me he was complimented by my attentions. I said, "You should be. Because you really did turn my head."

Oh sweet brat boy
Bellyward on my bed

And when the evening was ending, he said Cuca was jealous of me. I asked if she had said anything. He said no, but he can just tell. I asked what she was jealous about & he said, "She's afraid you're trying to turn me gay or something."

He keeps wearing the same shirt, but it always looks fresh on him. Somehow. In certain moments his hair looks like it could use a shampooing.

THOU HAST A SERPENT IN THINE HAIR

I asked if he read the poem & liked it. He hedged around, wouldn't be direct. I asked, "Did you *read* it?" He blurted out, "Yes, three times!" "And did you like it?" "Yes," he shouted, his eyes flashing proudly.

It seemed like every time he was on his way out, I was on my way in, and we'd bump into each other in the corridor.

In the beginning of the evening, I offered him a joint and he says, "Are you trying to get me stoned, Lou?" I laughed, "I'll try *anything*!"

MAI SCHWARTZ

we are better days

after Marsha Pisces

darling your DRESS makes me
want to do something intimate
like stealing
something
whose value only we
can perceive NOT a suitcase
full of money
more like
a couch DESIGNER meaning you
haven't heard but her vision changed
sitting
forever
darling your dress was MADE to be seen
on this sofa I'm ravished by the tableau
velvet plus
velvet plus
fringe equals STEEL you are a crime
against frugality the footsoldiers of decency
would die
to surrender before
dress me darling I'm hopeless a doll
with a juicy diaper RACING down my legs
a lush deformity
a profusion of luckless

keys spinning loosely in the nearest lock
be serious darling I BEG you
make me a late
in life bastard
I mean bachelor I mean hammered
in COPPER for the family crest
my cousin my co-chair
my friendly competition
it sucks how every faggot loves a fascist
or is one am I RIGHT let me die first
let the alley
keep the alley
and the aisle its slog to the sea
all roads may lead there but WHO said
go by road
or else
guess what girl we're GOING get in

MAXE CRANDALL

from Mud in Love

Scene 3: Yum Yum

MUD crawls into the mud pile for a hand-to-mouth feeding.
The monologue continues.

The people together the song I knitted

MUD has a bucket and in the bucket is a mud-like food. MUD picks some up on the ends of their fingers and eats a bite.

Let's slick our arms

MUD gets another bite.

Don't make hair

MUD takes another bite.

The scrawl is what we actually want

MUD gets another bite, pauses before they eat it.

this is what we eat in the dungeon

if it is a dungeon

in your terms what is a dungeon?

MUD eats it. MUD walks around with the bucket. Their gait makes you a little uncomfortable. Try not to laugh.

Yum Yum

Feeds it to someone.

Yum Yum

Feeds it to someone.

Yum Yum

Feeds it to someone.

Yum Yum

Feeds.

MUD walks from the people together back to the song. MUD knits its brow.

Ha.

Some people think I can't think

just because I don't have hair

I mean

I have hair in it

I have everything in it

MUD quietly puts the bucket down. New posture at an angle, shoulder against the wall.

What happened means I mourn

the mud I stopped

the mud I didn't stop

When someone gives you the mud

you should become it

MUD crawls around, collecting the shells on the floor. MUD puts them in a pile and stares at it for a while. Then MUD sits on a chair and crosses their legs. The next section is faster.

If only I could re-feel the love I felt

how many of us don't understand our love relationships

I should work it into my daily routine

My next move is a mouse

The number on the calling card was an elaborate sequence that lead me to

a tiny doorknob operating more like a button

In this day and age, deep within the lake

that vast body you may not recognize

is a submerged bottom known simply as mud

What the mud does is—

MUD picks a seam on the costume. The projection on the wall, to the left, begins.

Grounding. For you to know

that slickness stays

the grossness on your feet is a kind of beauty

that that that that

Mud is natural

and in this sense mud is social

it's something or someone

who will always sit down with you

Mud is a social act I mean mud is me

but what is mud what mud is being

in your minds

Getting angry now.

whose hands are always going in there for you

if you think you're so much better then tell me

what's at the bottom of you

do you even know what's in there

is the only way you can feel it

to throw it in the gutter

Back over to the shell pile. MUD deliberately crushes a few shells on the outside of the pile with their foot. Not an angry gesture, a sound.

now that we all have treats

we've given them to each other

that's what society is, right?

now that we have that

what will our adventure be?

MUD moves to the front of the space, closer to you.

The question now is what will you do with the mud?

MUD gets two sticks. One is short and thick; the other is long and a little thinner. MUD uses the short one to hammer a stone into the end of the long stick. The stone is shaped like a triangle. Now the long stick looks like an ax. MUD carries it over toward the wall and stops.

(as if the question suddenly occurs to them,)

If the whole world goes digital, what will happen to mud?

MUD hits the wall with the ax five times. The ax makes a very loud chopping noise when it hits the wall each time. MUD is more athletic than you probably expected. When they pull the ax back to strike, their body... torque. On the fifth strike, five longer wooden sticks fall from the ceiling to the floor.

There are some who believe that mud isn't animated

others who believe they are the first to have animated mud

to bring it to life?

to assert this kind of existence?

to begin to sell mud?

MUD picks up the six sticks one at a time. Each one fits into an invisible hole in the floor. MUD is working and building. Once the sticks are in their places, they form a circle around MUD. The two sticks in the middle, which MUD stands between, are taller than MUD.

The cultural fascination even obsession with mud

has to do obviously with romance

MUD slides the pile of shells into the circle. When some of the small shells fall out of the range of the force of MUD's hands, they go back and pick them up and bring them to the new location for the pile. The pile is near the middle but not in the middle. The projection swells. MUD looks out, straight ahead.

Mud is often used to build huts although it's difficult to give mud a shape without

water (1)
fire (2)
more dirt (3)
air (4)
sun (5)

What I'm trying to say this time is

suddenly there's a lot more mud

There's more of me than I'd accounted for

MILES COLLINS-SIBLEY

Mid-Morning Triptych

soft baby soft sheets the warmth left behind in the shape of a love left for another bathroom trip to come back only with cold feet. you didn't call, you didn't write. no, but i missed you and i brought you something. put cold feet against soft girl's warm stomach and the yelp. (i brought you that sound.) i brought you coming back to bed.

we have to get used to a new coffee color. we're switching to oat-milk. we're trying to admit a lactose intolerance born to brown skin. and by "we", i mean i. and i mean i have to get used to a cof-fee darker than the color of my own skin, sweet-ened with something not yet made on a plantation. is this a decolonization of my body? taking out milk bc by god i'm keeping cheese and sweetening with honey now (and the bees are disappearing.)

i'm drinking my coffee out of a mug i bought when my birth name was my first name and started with M and before the name i uncovered for myself started with A. and now both names are my middle names and my new name starts with M again. (being trans is hilarious. cis people make all the wrong jokes.) our wheat bread says no added nonsense and the second loaf in the freezer says, coldly, no added nonsense.

NAT RAHA

[second transfeminist tract / i]

galore in staying wake trill soft us
upon each suggest
to consider in pleasure
≠ before you/i draw sensate / quiet
streams to skin composed
&& arms around to dress ,,
pressing tangent/ temples & cheek\bone
\degrees 120 across neck in kiss:::y/our/s
sweet to musculature paths across\
that we invent passion here
in critique of universalisms,,,
that the labour to keep selves in
challenge of particulars our divergent bodies experience,,,
that to give hands // lips public to each
gains the signifier lesbian & politics is not a given,,,
that our genders socially contingent
& evolving in critique of the same,,,
that *inflammatory homosexual* is bracer rouse necessary
of desires we work to externalise from relational our;;

designation to us slipping enunciate relation adjective
accrued social form as image particular;
whereas *dyke bi punk riot drone sonics* does not
circulate the wealth does not on mainstations we

speak in thrills relative ~~ff~~ by
flesh temperate for arms softkiss before
timepolitik construes AM upon plural
that we will be tired in hours free from our wage work /
left to domestics
„ you holding & close \ shoulder to
button print resist psychic death

(when we're working while we're asleep)

curves us from
the day's intern
\ positioned , close drawn
, heat
wrap shift
affections 'cross
surfaces

our,

cheek &
hairstroke comfort in
the
historicity of rest space ::
keeps minds near [Δ
& felines in start: winter
, radiates through privacy housed, exchanged,
captures each action for
& emits social myth [§ & that
if restless
we will
struggle at the premise capacity for the day due
/ as the blind pulls itself
to gloam

electric the police stationed/ fortifies
neighbourhood ≠

of arms tending , clutch
despite the nerves inactive , ache
limbs to agony / drained from the type,
inhabits exiting to a.m., alarmist // held
together queer women
anterior to labour dates /
subsist even as muscles &
/or thought stall
:: without of the workplace forms
as it shores subjection / cultivates , gains our
remaking out of sight // that
the fictitious private, hewn their
reified work of romance
the relations where our genders fall
as the simplest of words, we
lust for the rest / hands
freest from repetitions of the wage

, they: pathology weaponised
struggle to thieve health / to grasp the poem
& nuzzle you as capital kisses it night

from [9x9]

[2]
decimate, un/made & horny
, our shaven flesh & locks, dined on
black beans, corn & sugar, *vagabonds,*
tinkers, tricksters & jailbirds <
had demanded our bodies o
fascist rags, codes & division
s systematic flesh & capitals

nostalgia imposed & gen
der/ivative nations ,, soil f~

[5]
grrrl // if we are citizens
of nowhere, a threat to the tone &
image;; composed / lace cute
we divine femmes no here to dissect
your impositions >> bark organs
so late in the day, directions
on casual violence: if your pleasure
excruciate living / &
the beauty about our eyelines

[8]
at the trial of yur crimes of invention
in my charred golden minidress /
cremated homes, debt && circuits
capital commission & hate

dined on flour, divine salt &&
threads of your flags ,, aroused,
our vulgar comedy, drives &
erotics silenced ~~>/ your~~ beliefs
& rituals :: disintegrating, foxed

[ii/3]
we, the invisible: streets strewn
w/ feathers, our solitude
-- negative reveries vibrant
squatting schools & rulings, yur
nights ripped by fire, disinvest
-ed / the deepened particular
of fleshes, our / memory embodied
, itching, wet on the union jack
your truths will be rerooted--

ing in the dream
etters, archive
ose hip flesh d
ge creopolitan

sleeve stitched bare
what waking ca , tended, strapp
type
ar-

beau-
is odily
e bitch be ared colour s
h potential fagg try,, the
ades pressed you

e ga us pre/ten
anthropos
d vulnerabil
er wha

[ii/7]
bred throug , th
-lar, our t preo
remain ake, sign co
you/ bare hands & fr zing
ks talen : glam/o
orget the legi
& diminished

NATALIE MESNARD

Projection in Retrograde

Scorpio, it's time for contemplation.
Hear this: my life has been a hologram.
History has no mirror but stars misaligned,
a thousand tessellated lichens
and I have been trying to read them. I admit,
a peculiar astrology: girl, boy, body
as brown moth come to rest
in the lee of an I. Magnetism is forecast.
You may force a silk rose through one eye
of the 3D moving image. And
when Justin Timberlake brings sexy back
at summer's bravura performance,
some rosé-all-day DIY backyard wedding
you may—no, you will—go get down.
Say of the synth pink thread
coming through the I it's made of stone.
Stone from which hangs stones,
grave markers wearing tessellated lichens.
The pattern gets so misaligned. Please,
Scorpio, read this horoscope sober
as a moth. My whole life has been a hologram.
A history of body as bangled, begging
hand. But you, you're down to reflect
on what you're transmitting, aren't you?
Or what did you mean when, leaving
advice in the guestbook that evening, drunk
on your own stars, notion of goodbye
you wrote, *wear each other's clothes*?

That night,
It was raining I was walking I was texting
in the rain I was sending I was running into the question
text messages and trying to skirt Times Square
I was wet here was my nonbinary friend
I was raining texting
checking Instagram
here was my blonde friend are you trans?
are
at Mean Girls on Broadway
you
I walked in the rain raining?
she had a sweet, cold are
you at Mean Girls
summer I was raining on
Broadway in Times
here was my scientist friend
asking had I finished editing
the paper on
exploratory data analysis what is
emergent
she was happy in her body he was
happy in his analysis
the blonde was nonbinary the scientist

was texting
to be at Mean Girls on Broadway in Times are we
Square I kept running into the
Square?
he had a sweet, cold question
I was walking in the rain
water I was studying
the clustering
pink lights yellow lights purple lights
space

stop

I walked past
Mean Girls on Broadway in Times Square
it was pink I wasn't happy in my body
light a coincidence in my
analysis
it was circumstance but I lived it and
QED sweet, cold
I was (un)happy in my analysis I mean because
I didn't have one.
we were all there

NM ESC

Sunset Vans

i.

sunset songs queue on the aux / we drive through magic hour / & it makes our faces round & golden / our voices take the shape of different roads.

in the morning we hear that the government is shutting down & we hope they mean for good /& we rejoice / because we used to think there could be art warm enough to melt the knots of hate out of the body politic / but now we know / this country was built rotten / stayed rotten the whole way through

what i am saying is i feel helpless every day & now we have this van & if there wasn't so much work to do we could just drive it straight into a canyon & live slow. what i am saying is i still feel most at home up & down an open interstate / & i could use that calm to spread / because there is so much to hold / & i have such strange dreams here.

ii.

the sun is setting on the porch / short / like summer camp is short & afterwards / some kids go back to sunlight & we go back to asphalt / & a sharp season / in which we break ourselves open / & mop each other up / until we are covered in each other's wetness / until we all smell of copper / & ash

the sun is setting & i want to start smoking again. the sun is setting & my friend just changed her gender marker because she is afraid of ending up in the wrong prison / & all prison is the wrong prison / but we still celebrate.

like in philly i'm lying with jacky & the dog watching the gay ice skater anime when they say, *there are material consequences for living how we do*. or in richmond dandy reminds me / how this winter we wrapped our friendships around us so tightly they tore at the seams / & called it a suicide watch / & sobbed into wet sandwiches when the healthcare system couldn't hold us right / or under streetlights / when our lovers wouldn't hold us right / or by the cemetery / with the precipice so close.

iii.

i'm terrified that the summer beat us home. down here the summer settles easy—gentle on the porch, jurassic landscape. we wake up when the sun is high enough to warm us.

i'm getting sentimental / lingering / like how the sun gets so caught up in hair / like staying close so as not to break this forcefield / like, sorry if this is boring but i love this song

the mid atlantic's cursed / so much death stretches up & down i-95 & still we stretch towards each other / state by state / vertebrae by vertebrae

lana is singing *'a lust for life' (a lust for life) 'keeps us alive' (keeps us alive)* & that better be enough because soon we won't afford our meds. or, vitamin c is singing / *say it right now cuz you won't get another day*. but why not / could she know / that past the carbon crisis point even the ocean's trying to come for us / like, could she know / the heat / will push out all the air / & i will hold my breath / each time a friend walks home alone in a statement heel

the sunrise creeps / blue and austere like this motel room / threadbare like sleep

if property is theft and theft is proper then i'm going to put my fist right through the sun and pull the light out. because we didn't choose or want these bodies /

but we are losing the right to repair them / & we need that warmth to hold each other up

if property is theft and theft is holy then i am proud / of every single year we've stolen back / of how much joy / is possible / to haul away from here / before the fuckers catch us.

black cars gather sun. black shirts in summertime. a burn

starts as an itching. dragonflies like tiny helicopters, circling.

back in the city these shapes would be drones. after bean's memorial

we sat by the river watching the helicopters land.

shared a sandwich. could use a sandwich now.

REGULATION PENETRATES
INTO THE SMALLEST DETAILS

i (beg for months then) never pick the script up

EVERY POSSIBLE   TRANSMITTED
WHEN BODIES ARE MIXED TOGETHER.

lines in the sand / each line becomes a wall. compassion

& revenge. what if we scorch the archive? get lower, dirtier.

come back covered in dirt. the child that wanders off

into the woods returns part animal. & then the slaughter.

turn all the kids to dust. & then the phoenix

Born:2

fireflies flood the valley
flash flood warning not enough
to scare from seeking shelter in
communal ambiance embrace
& hold

r, slammed up against the wall
by f's ghost on the dance floor:
"pay yr respects goddammit"
in tribute of piss, tribute of cum
in tribute: blood scratched ink
& heaviest of all: tribute of tears

we said what can we do to help
she said just hold me
so we did

pulled out & pushed into
where spider bodies kansas crawl the pit
thrown into sibling arms that catch you
bruised & wailing: soaked

like, lightness my old friend
broke through to daybreak, so

in tears again: a feelings-wet
in parallel to leather, latex
glove-wet : slide : in bond
& opening

i missed yr mouth i stuffed
a crush letter / heart-deco / crushed into:
i wrote each of my friends a love letter

& swung into the morning as the dj wrapped,
hands still inside each other clawing
towards weightlessness

(against weight of betrayal: all this wasted time:

we mercenary jumped to kill
the parts of us they needed dead

but here:

re: animated / splendent
here: in full monstrosity
& loved

NOAH LEBIEN

Big Dick Plague

my dick is so much
bigger than yours
as you're fucking me in the ass
on the spectral plane of a kind of
hardcore world, abusing ourselves
for revulsion and revolt, entering gory erotic states
to roll back the intestines
of the mother goddess
into her gaping mouth
because gaping is Good, openness to all experience
 through sex karma, sucking on bad omens
and pentagrams that circulate like air
in the new pagan economy, blissful interpenetration
of existence in all the
living deferred from us
before ur-deviant prophecy:
two bodies
        make up a pit,
        an allfather goes in,
        the seed becomes a shower—
thus begins the struggle,
as the gas starts to envelope us
from the Horsehead nebula, shrieks come in indigo
of being

forced to find limitless
ways to waste time
in the macho-logical world, tired of not existing
so fucking a path through, finding the perfect wound,
waiting for this beautiful
  cocktail of seeds, pumpkin, semen and cumflower and sun, sun
    to go airborne
    and end the whole war

The Last One

we dream of titanic interplanetary
barge ships hauling shit of
offworld tyrannical warlords into
the heart of the sun, having won capitalism
through wormholes, their waste rains over us
which is what it feels like
in this city and why i can't see you
moist lump of underwear, which was probably urine??
our hands met like
buttercup yellow to the flower, i've got
so much consent to give, too much, too much...
in the bellies of those who starved
and did have to eat heroin needles
under blackened skies, on the days it's harder to remember   yes, people really
will do
the most horrifying things
just to feel connected with each other
and right now i'm unlearning
the thought that what i've got can be cured
so is it
zen to do drag or not? the opposite of emptiness
warring with the elements
instead of white men
with tiny limp cocks   1 billion of us, alone on a planet of trash

covered in blue urine
given us from the clouds, from worship of
condom-slick hemicycles
we'd have sheepskin condoms for skin, black seed tampon
and rain surrogates   wait a second, oh
i actually really fucking care about you
i made myself forget because
you're on a different planet, in a zoo
in neon stasis, in a casket with pulsating limbs
and i've come to rescue you   stowed in the cargo
because no one will believe
how much the poem will be known in the future life
as an ancient attempt
at explaining
the biopsionic love we feel for each other, which propagates
like a soundwave
across oceans and oceans of space time and us alone

NORA FULTON

The proprietor of the bicycle shop leads a normal life until he starts repeatedly getting called to jury duty in Paris. His obsession with finding his customers the perfect bicycle becomes an obsession with justice. But a man keeps coming to the shop wanting to make certain exchanges. First, he asks to exchange the tandem bicycle that he bought for his fiancée for two bicycles, so that they can each have one – their relationship has dissolved. Later, he asks to exchange his single bicycle (what he kept of the pair) for the same tandem he'd traded, because he met someone new and they're to be married any day now. The proprietor is clearly an affable and romantic person who defines himself by his capacity for hospitality, so he allows the exchange to be made and warmly congratulates the man on finding new love. After another call away to the courts, the proprietor returns to find the man back again with his quote-unquote new tandem, wanting to exchange it for another two bicycles. Another relationship dissolved. The trade takes place once more, with a bit more chagrin this time on the part of the proprietor, and of course this cycle repeats once more due to our obsession with 'the third time.' (Things have to happen three times to bear power as analogies: one leaves us hungry/horny, two pales in comparison to the first, and three secures the first as nostalgia and second as exactly what we deserved.)

At least for a while we can think about the flat tension between ideas of justice and hospitality here, of equal and unequal exchanges. But everything is ruined if we discover that the man was actually selling off the second bicycle he would always have left over from the trade – a revelation no doubt rooted in the 20th century decision for inhospitable justice over unjustified hospitality; a revelation no doubt rooted in the 20th century decision for the inequality of both equal and unequal exchanges; a revelation no doubt rooted in the 20th century obsession with locating the sucker. These are decisions that emerge from a singular desire to 'not have been had.'

The actual results of each court case are insignificant, though the proprietor treats them with the utmost seriousness, and you can see the evolution of his sense of justice as his hospitality is progressively tested back at the shop. (At first he lets the accused off easy; soon enough he wants them degraded and destroyed.) What matters is that both 'the just one' and 'the hospitable one' are starting points for this image of the social, and can seemingly choose themselves, create themselves out of nothing, in order to disprove their origin in the sucker. And of course this image is utterly untenable, because both giving hospice and finding justice require a total elision of the host and the judge, of that person's pride. They require that one is always 'having been had.' Think of someone describing the one who falls for a grift as having been 'taken in.' Taken in by what is not immediately present in what is presented to us: we find shelter and survival, are taken in, not by what we agree to, but by the place in which we agree. So, given outcome of the proprietor's participation in the final trial, at the center of which figures a brutal knife murder, we can truly say that there is a history in philosophy rather than a history of philosophy: a history of the displacement of the indefinite repetition of a null trace whose effects are real.

Suqu

I was working at the franchise I've never worked at, the one they carved into the art-deco train station that my landlord remembers as grassland. It was late at night, the weather was shit, I was closing, and I got this joint text from another trans girl I know and another trans girl I don't really know; she is a minor online celebrity, which seems so common. 'That which is most common is most rare,' and so on. The message was written by the girl I do know, and it read something like: "we were going to say hi, because ____ and I were talking about what you and I had talked about that time, about suqu. Neither of us claim to experience what you claim to experience, but we both struggle with suqu occasionally. It arises out of nothing and is uncontrollable, like a neighbourhood." For context, the girl I do know told me once that her transition feels basically over, that if she were born AFAB she would have ended up a trans man. The girl I don't know will start transitioning next year and passes better than any cis woman who has ever lived. I love them both, but we have little in common in terms of our transness, so suqu couldn't have to do with that. The text finished, "so we don't need a drive. xo, ____ and ____. Oh, and we were waving at you at the checkout, did you see us?" I lied and said I didn't.

I closed the franchise and took this long flat black box out from under the till and put it in my car, and the five blocks on the way back to my house became a series of winding off-ramps and alleys, hazy in the drizzle. I couldn't stop wondering what suqu meant, and kept noticing at the last minute that I was about to take a turn too wide, which led to me jumping the car up onto shimmering sidewalks, then trying to pull it back, the weight of each turn the only thing I had to work with, the swerve glossier than usual, the mist falling in blue sheets. At my apartment, there was a dinner party going on. The light music and soft clamour of people was all around me, and the rent was due. I stood the long flat black box upright below the slatted window. The people who were and weren't there totally accepted my presence, welcomed me, but I was distracted. I tried to think of everything I'd said to ____ and ____ – in that strange form of trans temporality both of them are much younger than me, but having transitioned earlier, also much older – and I couldn't remember coming up with some nonce term like suqu to describe something that, years later, would probably seem like the most obvious and oft-restated component of a world that was, at the point when I had coined it, more unknown than I knew, and deserved a term that constituted more than the entirety of my descriptive capabilities. I was sure I hadn't coined it and would never coin it. As soon as I woke up the next morning I searched the word and could find nothing; or rather, I found any number of irrelevant meanings, because language rarely helps. I wanted to go back to sleep, but couldn't, and then could.

NORA TREATBABY

Ammo In Hairdo

as the indifference collapses
what do I lack
clover askance
perceptions dribble in avowed closet of reason
this subject is my permanence stage
womanness through which an image can mature
but that's not where I will stay
abandoned in normative poetry
the dream of coherence
survival is chasing me like a cop
which caption would you prefer
probably a life
no change in transmission
theory floats in and out of utter identity
you will feel like vast wilderness feels as it is being imagined

I need someone to hold my stupid hand   I seething
located where I occulent is
lesbionic dementia
arrange me next to
you- her- flowers- so I can be a pretty thing
worth culled from
the field of revolt I cute
I settle into my glass hole
with one good lantern and a polemic
I move closer to
inquisitiveness and grade into arrangement
always walking back into itself
a grid of mirrors
the information in
genitals follows logic to grave dug in unsexed trance
so I can land this plane of babies
the regarded flesh burns outward the
disturbance of prosperity in aperture

I am the vice versa of I today
voice operates in reflex
attempting to swim out of the liminal fractal
of explanation my enemy is suede
noun choreography
isn't flow
my eros needs housing
field of tension
pleasure dimensions act filling the send up that calls
backwards to city burnt where we will careen
into the disrobement machine
morning littles the canvas like a pearl
inch removed between two instruments
I name me but you inscribe my shape informally

PEACH KANDER

try

after Dennis Cooper

Friday again
I bulldoze into open space
like a goldfish
my perfect ske|eton
reads: handle with care
please come
make me double - jointed
the honey in my cupboard
is crystallized & sour
an odor   beneath   the skin
I watch: the peaches
burst Open in the Sun
fuzz caking to smoke
letting the mold [set]
to make sweeet things tru-er
my teeth ~ a preview
if you know where to peel
my perfect skeleton
spine !ike a !eash
the collar should be *tighter*
if I'm still siingiing
wake me up

You could be on the toilet scrolling through
the apps like a catalogue, the humans
staged in the photos as stand ins for
brand, disposition. After sneaking its
way through the plumbing like it's the loop de
loop on top of your childhood hamster's
cage it pops out, through your detritus
escaping from the porcelain vessel.
You're horrified, though not entirely
surprised, as this is a phenomenon
you've read about, too much even perhaps
such is your lack of shock. Think of other
peoples' stories, like your friend who was
on the subway platform glancing sideways
/
A rat, its obsidian beads, met her
gaze and charged. They say there are ones in parks
as big as possums, toddlers. An acrid smell
around the station, for in this quest to
eradicate or control the rat, they're
willing to take us all out. Like if we live
at all, we can live without them. I've had rats
in my walls, scratching back and forth to each
other when we couldn't sleep. Boxes poisoned

and baited on almost every corner
every stoop, outside the deli
full of cats, to stop what will be here
even after we all leave, running
a rat along the third rail, unabashed

RACHEL FRANKLIN WOOD

MUD EFFIGY

Necessarily mud dries to rigor mortis, so Golem commits herself to the new science of arteries. Of course, this comes with the requisite failures. Any son implanted with a soaker hose under his skin looks as if he's just escaped the aggression of a large and cruel-growing animal, exertion and bluster and weeping brown tears from every inch of his body.

Sweat, she says, lightly running two fingers across her boy's brow with the wistful deliberation of an antiquer in his childhood bedroom, realizing old belongings boast the right patina to spruce up a window display off a once quiet main street giving way now to gentrification, *just sweat*. But her boy is convinced that in him something is broken and has always been and asks her to examine his teeth for hairlines.

One morning, she wakes to find a clipping from the school newspaper taped to the refrigerator. *DO YOU KNOW THE SIGNS OF FRACKING?* it asks. She doesn't. *WOULD YOU LIKE TO?* it asks.

1. A CREEPING FEELING THAT LARGE MEN IN DIRTY TANK-TOPS ARE MEETING JUST BEYOND THE PROPERTY LINE TO DISCUSS YOUR IMMEDIATE FUTURE.
2. FIRES IN ALL THE WRONG PLACES. THE SINGLE BUSH BESIDE THE MAILBOX MIGHT GO UP FAST AND YOU WON'T GET THERE IN TIME TO SAVE IT.
3. ONCE BENIGN HOLES IN THE GROUND SWALLOWING YOU WHILE

YOU SLEEP. (DO NOT EXPECT TO BE SPIT BACK UP)
4. A SUDDEN INFLUX OF INCOME (E.G. CASH) AND/OR DESPAIR (E.G. CASH).

Golem follows a fresh set of muddy footprints from kitchen, to threshold, to driveway, to the stranger standing with his back to her—a white hard hat, a hole in blue sky—squinting at the last bit of wet trickling down her ravine.

I guess we were wrong, ma'am, the hard hat says, *about there being any oil here.* He has coiled the soaker hose and is wearing it as a sash around his chest. She can't tell him it belongs to her.

And she won't, even as her boy's armature is dropped body heavy in the back of the company truck and the hard hat trades presence for a cloud of agitated silt in the air. A voice from the stir comes ghostly back, says, *ma'am*, says, *I'd recommend spraying down the road—*

says, *imagine me dust-lost, found in the ditch.*

RAQUEL SALAS RIVERA

soon we'll be people again

west philly summer 2018

so hot you want to
shave your eyebrows group ice
in a sock

and break the slick
off the glass

pour out the air that's trapped
in all the cupboards called stores distance
the drinks from faucets divvy up the water

ride waves of some glimpsed
hell scarred backwards into its
opposing linger

you come down cussing out the sun
spitting up red through the light
leveling out the rage

hot so

you dip your face in icecream pools lap
up the cracks

ant corpses littering playgrounds dying
dried-out on jungle gyms half
crossed sliding
into dead sparrows

hot enough to harbor a grudge
head out to sea to show
up at the wrong door with a timber and a fuck you

when you see a mail truck and think

it's a whale

carcass holding in leagues
of carved out faces you imagine ghosts

grooming plastic plants
daliesquescapes into brick-hunting insoles and
every corner store waves
a white flag called *we sell ice summer is*
a luxury season

hot

going to hold it down block by
block the earworm that sweats
into sputtering a desire to spit at

every white question
every nice house with a.c. clean lawns sprinkled
dreams of buyé out in the open

i'm not from here so gimme a minute
to remember streams enough to make do locking

into the overture a chipped-toothed sun laughing
through a heavy cloud still

hot but could be rain and
stuck in a noon dodging
in to buy our way through degrees
of lessening sudden cut

and honk of a delivery gone awry from festered
flashes of a memory tank barging wood

sinister in its splintering age should be
better than metal but
only the fireflies know we
mean to leave this planet

until someone brings water

you can't decide if beer is
what we need just to numb through yellow

discus thrown out into the trash heavens
as if we were cursed
to live this out until we can heal it or
repay winter we tremble

in thirst
as if wishing a downpour from our
bodies out into
the symmetry of water just above the road

seeing things
seething things or

broken on hubs in a park
promising relief tree-ridden
sick with green heavy onwards

trapping mosquitoes against thighs
a sacrifice for night

saying bring it down into
the insole of a bold-faced lie called
we're cool

not today
or ever
again going to be a cold bone between us sarcophagi

we call litmus of all other hatreds the belly of the earth
much better the pig in the mud of this body cooling off
in a shade
rasping its skin off on the bark

until breaking into the flesh
of it ray by ray
the divided seconds
of day of it
unsustainable and fountain-bound

heading into the fray
holding on by dear cube shirt high or
off into the shrubs

packing corners with unused lengths

i say *soon we'll be people again i promise*

we'll order in and return
to mimicking survival to our slow declines

and handheld hopes sort of not
knowing how to wield them but still battling away

from wrist flicking out gesturing at
waterfalls pools

icebergs melted into things we can eat
or drink or dribble as if talking
but really what i say is *soon we'll be people again*

and no one is listening from however we aren't
ice arrests the usual called making it matter hot
in cages
in el yunque bald-headed
across the beach of my past stretched out

my body of water
my mountainous descent into the city
and the coast of a city hit by rivers where
swimming is ill-advised
secretly thinking
soon

we'll be better
than the people we were
better than summer
we'll be scattered showers
we'll be sun-down and broken
a headstone struck by its own force
rivulets across its cracked face
taking us over

RAY FILAR

You've heard of Ritalin, now what if I told you governments make bodies into crime scenes for no reason at all

[extract]

1. The process speeds up when they finally say you've got it. The ADHD drug methylphenidate, aka Concerta, aka Ritalin, is a psychostimulant, much like amphetamine, aka speed, and much like meth-amphetamine, aka crystal meth. There are chemical differences, of effect, of intensity, but the real difference is whether your worst encounter is tabloid denigration, or whether it's jail time for possession. This shows that there are two correct ways to take stimulants: either with medical approval, after a psychiatrist confirms you have the right kind of brain abnormality, or by being white and rich enough to not get caught.

//

3. Drugs are not just chemicals; they name a politics. They carry feelings, weight, which is why they call it getting loaded. They sit symbolically at the centre point of a distributed swirl of affect, what Sara Ahmed calls 'affective economies', in which 'sticky words' glue emotions to concepts, to people, therefore to groups,

both psychically and socially. Some drugs are stickier than others: crystal meth is sticky, the ADHD drug methylphenidate merely slippy. White peoples' recreational drug use is an issue of health, people of colours' recreational drug use is a sign of the criminal, the threatening.

This politics shapes the world to a ruling class vision. The fantasy 'drugs' fabricates enemies of the state, while psychoactive chemicals–taking them or struggling to get them–keep people compliant.

All things are chemicals, really, but some of them are more so.

Pharmaceutical drugs produce workers, as they regulate workforces. Pharmaceuticals produce tranquility, a self-imposition of the sedate. And consistent productivity, often, mandates drug use.

For the last decade I've held various self-employed, usually precarious writing jobs. In the morning I wake up and I have no desire to do any work whatsoever, in fact the idea of work is preposterous, it's sickening. Nobody would choose to do it, there is TV to watch, books to read, there is morning meandering, there is the window to stare through. I drink an earl grey tea, I take a methylphenidate. I sit at my desk. Work, in varying forms, happens; it happens to me, whether through guilt or sheer force of repetition. By 4pm my heart races, the methylphenidate causing nervous peaks and troughs reminiscent of ecstasy. Sometimes I take a propanalol, an anti-anxiety drug which slows the action of adrenaline in the body. My stomach unclenches. I am able to work. I feel a sense of achievement. By 7pm I'm strung out, tetchy, as the daily methylphenidate comedown hits. I move onto wine to get me over the hump. This works very well. Having not had the money to buy a proper desk and chair, I wake up with back pain, sometimes it's hard to move. I take two ibuprofen. I ask my partner to put deep heat on my back. I obediently perform the litany of stretches the osteopath tells me to perform. They seem to work, but never completely. In my bag I carry: methylphenidate, ibuprofen, paracetamol, cigarettes, propanalol, anti-indigestion drugs, anti-diarrhoea drugs. In my desk drawer: valium, tramadol, G, a packet of 2CB that I'm not taking because last time it was unpleasant and the neighbours wouldn't stop playing music while I was trying to experience a state of complete internality.

Drugs name a politics of usage: the sanctioned chemical usage that produces work or reproduces the workforce, and those whose chemical usage reproduces a class of non-workers, the prison force, the unemployed, the 'junkie', those for whom usage becomes a social marker of fear or degradation.

And sometimes drugs produce resistance, the capacity to imagine rebellion.

4. If you are assigned the label 'female' at birth, it takes a regular 10 minute GP appointment to get a National Health Service (NHS) prescription for oestrogen and progesterone. If you are assigned 'male' at birth and are considered to have 'low' testosterone, you can buy it on the internet.

The NHS trans medical pathway means you have to wait a year to several years for hormones considered of the 'other gender'. This is purposeful. It's about what's allowed to be 'real'. Cis women's reproductive capacities are real, controlled towards or away from fertility along racial lines. Angela Davis, drawing on the example of the US during the 1970s, describes the ways in which 'women of color are urged, at every turn, to become permanently infertile,' while 'white women enjoying prosperous economic conditions are urged, by the same forces, to reproduce themselves'.[2] Rich white cis men are not only real but define who else is allowed to be, and how.

Trans people are not real, in fact we are violent, illusory, delusional, lying, sick and pretending, and so cannot decide for ourselves. Keep the transes fighting for shorter waiting times to enter their preferred place in the gender binary; hamstring a radical movement. Keep the potential destabilisers destabilised. This is why AFAB people can have oestrogen on the NHS but trans women can't, cis men can have testosterone from the internet but trans men can't. Non-binary people don't exist at all and therefore can't have anything from anyone.

2 p.365, Angela Davis, Women, Race and Class.

I have waited four years, not for an official medical prescription for T, but for a conversation in which I try to prove I deserve it. 'She wants to be they', I picture a psychiatrist writing, dismissively, 'No real need for treatment'.

//

6. The same summer I self-medicate T-gel, the ex who broke my heart messages me. We haven't spoken for two years, but now he's lonely. With equal amounts of optimism and annoyance, I text back. The first night he stays over at mine, we lie, bodies pressed length to length on the cracked brown pleather sofa in my living room. He's improbably beautiful, his jaw all perfect angles, effortlessly tousled hair, one of those indisputable faces, the kind that throughout our relationship had drawn repetitive congratulation from friends on my proximity to such aesthetic success. He knows this, too, and though I veer between envy and disbelief I think his self-knowledge is feminist. Unexpectedly, his body is a homecoming. 'I still love you', I confess, acknowledging the coursing excitement I feel at having him in my arms. This careens from the stereotypically lesbian to the openly pathetic, but it's fine, I tell myself, lesbianism dies hard and boys have feelings too.

Placatory, my ex says he loves me as well. He explains he has the capacity to fall in love with lots of different people, with most women, probably. Its unclear whether this is an admirable open-heartedness, a pure polyamorous capacity to see the virtue in anyone, or rather, I suspect, a flattening of love's hard specificity. My ex might love anyone, it's possible I might love just him. We used to be a dyke couple, now, we joke, we're just two friendly guys hanging out in bed laughing, roleplaying heterosexual male homoeroticism for kicks, making out, but definitely not having sex, because that would make things too official. We call each other bro in a way that is kind of a joke, but also kind of not a joke. No/so homo.

//

14. Here's how it goes. In mid-2015 I visit my local South London GP and ask for a referral to the Gender Identity Clinic. Four years later, I have made ten increasingly reluctant visits to chase the referral. Each time, a new doctor, the

curiously neutral look of the prurient but trained professional: does this she want to be a he? Why? Four years of recounting, to demand, the trans trauma of an obedient animal. Trans subjects are constituted by perseverance, but also though the confession of trauma. Unhappiness is a prerequisite of transition. In this way the deviant body is medicalised into the compliant capitalist subject.

I met someone once who regretted transitioning, the media chorus confides, and now: the horror...mannish tone...mutilated chest... irreversible...

The GP has read about people like me, but not really. I lower my voice and monitor my body language for disqualifying femininity. Each ten minute appointment, from the beginning, I regurgitate my explanation for being trans, as if an explanation is possible, my reasons for wanting a referral to medical intervention, as if a cisgender doctor who has just met me could, in ten minutes, have any meaningful insight into the condition of 'alienated by patriarchy, but in a trans way'. A year and a half after the first appointment I have blood tests taken and deposited neatly into the ether, never to be heard from again. My blood pressure is monitored. The third doctor acknowledges that my first two requests have resulted in no action. The next sends the referral letter to a place that doesn't exist. Further doctors fail to chase this. I write a lengthy formal complaint, which disappears. I don't know who to follow up with. In 2017 I stop going to the doctor. I get ill and deal with it by myself. I start going to the doctor again, through sheer force of stubbornness. The referral is dropped, then picked up again by a visibly exhausted but well-meaning GP I've never met before. I change address, and they write down the wrong new address for me, so for six months I do not get any letters. In 2018 I start refusing to talk in detail to the GPs about why I want the referral, saying that I will speak further at the Identity Clinic itself: my medical records note that the trans patient refuses to answer questions, though, the record clarifies, I am not aggressive about it. Would being more aggressive speed things up? Make me more male? Somehow trans masc aggression is both more punished and more ridiculous.

...How awful, replies the happily grimacing public imaginary, can I see pictures?...

Meanwhile, for laughs, I fight both the gendered administration of the surgery and my own ADHD, which makes persistence in the face of transphobic bureaucracy unbelievably difficult. The first question on the surgery check-in touch-screen: choose between a blue figure in trousers or a pink figure in a triangle dress. Of course, sour-faced, I select neither. The receptionist knows me and visibly scowls when I walk into the surgery, she thinks I'm a dick. She might be right. I am rude and uppity and forever causing a bureaucratic fuss in a waiting room full of sick people with real problems. It's not cancer, is it, it's selecting a symbolic colour on a screen. I shift into avoidance mode, six months later, with renewed optimism, I attempt to re-register my name on the NHS system, to use the title Mx, to avoid having letters sent or prescriptions made out to the dead name I stopped using over a decade ago. My passport is not enough. My deed poll, brought in, scanned, is not enough, though NHS guidance says it should be. I bring both in several times, timing my visits around this cycle of resentful executive dysfunction.

The administrative staff revolt: a jobsworth transphobe called Christine telephones me, speaks slowly to me as though I am very unwell, tries to convince me out of this lunacy. She tells me that to use my actual name and Mx. I must re-register as male on the NHS, though, she warns me in a low, coaxing whisper, that means I won't get letters regarding cervical smears or breast cancer (if only, I think, the act of registering as male would be enough to make breasts or cervixes disappear). I wonder why I must be officially male to use a gender neutral title. I wonder if women who change their names post-marriage have to bring in deed polls for suspicious-eyed scrutiny.

...Eventually...you'd never know!...(But, the chorus whispers, how do they have sex?)...

'No one will know', says Christine on the phone, 'no one will know if you just stay female'. 'I will know', I reply, spluttering. A year later I drag myself in again, try not to cry, fill in a re-registration form, defiantly mark it both male and non-binary, tick the 'other' title box. Christine refuses the form, sends another to my house with the note: 'Ray, just tick M or F and get this back to us.' After four years I change doctors. Its 2020. I am still waiting.

This is how we constitute gender through cultural legibility; alternatives are written out through sheer admin. My even writing this story connotes a certainty that I don't feel, an endpoint I'm not sure about.

//

16. At a follow up appointment I lightheartedly tell Daddy psychiatrist that the ADHD meds make alcohol feel more intense, more potent. Immediately, he's suspicious, eyes tight behind his glasses. As if perhaps the definition of abuse is to combine a prescribed drug with a legal one, or like perhaps it's my fault that the effects last all day. The body processes the meds and the drinks in the same way, he barks; he's only looking out for my liver. He gives me a tight follow up prescription, suddenly I might be a wayward drug abuser rather than a legitimate daily meds user, one a day and we'll see you at the end of the month, no room for additional snorting; I'm a teen behind the bike shed or a bottom rung city banker sweating through my Jermyn Street collar. In his suspicion there is unexpressed fear: that sanctioned therapeutic use might be an unstable category, in need of protection from the gateway to meth-head, system-gamers like me, who need to be watched for their own good.

Maybe I should stop drinking, Daddy psychiatrist suggests. That's not realistic, I say, thinking: bro, you are literally giving me speed, and it's not lost on me that this is only legally ok because the pills mean I can do my job better, its as if David Cameron told me to put on a proper tie and I said yes, fantastic, I'll pay £18 a month for it.

ROCKET CALESHU

FEYE

I eye u first & hardest in the clipped
slide between sanguine and shroud
/between zero and the abyss
/between acker and right now
/between a dime and one hundred
/between #same and ruin
/between glance and chaos
Vibration of yr thick eyelashes
moving in unison like the long hand
of a broken clock

bouncing b/w two seconds
When the blink reeach rrreach reetches\
our silent dialogue oils yr grip
on my throat. *Dare a me,*

time boiled into submission
[steel persists gaze persists]
Too thick to ignore,

I separate yr lashes
w/ my tongue one at a time,
cleansed by the looking itself
Face 2 face w/ an other animal,

sweating supplants thought

:If the expanse we face isn't empty
we 2 range as organisms of plunge we are

:If a 1st conversation, gently lapping
language barriers, then a single glass

tear rolls down time's babyface:
Posso vedere? Of course u can &
blast the findings on repeat <infinity sign>

2 x beasts in the darkness, one animal
synthetic and one still becoming but
all kinds of shot up and inverted 2
Moving delinquent against incalculable

shores, flung hard into each//other
geographies complexed infinitely

Maketh me mine bless'd mirror of
taxonomy. crawl & bounce sissy into
labor of can't stay still but still come
from somewhere *have to come from*
somewhere Leave me in yr ruined cave
of utopia shrieking and shin'd or j
get in my whip.

I'm betrothed to movement
Movement
under cover of night
under cover of skin
        <can't see what happens
        under this flesh or yrs but>

roiling frothing evanescent fields of being
(a posteriori experience of ID's liquidation)

Dawn and decomposition almost visible
in perma-gloam of touch
Twisting into my shape 4 u:
tangere tangere tangere

Clotted w/ our own fullness, running our
fingers through vines, you dragging me
limpwrist'd thru the dirt, absence of echo,
absence of floor. Nature's not natural
but blindfolded by wildness:

Why when I press on yr orbitals they
don't burst. Are ribs bones? Knees suggest
they elastic under my caps, humor in
bruised form – new kind of sublime,
rich w/ its own brevity, blossoms
around your hand
<back in the dirt ascending>

My flies for eyes rub their legs together
x-wise, suggestive. Hear their blistering
song calling u across the Expanse
a contracting/dilating lung sac
sirening our degradation,,
always for pleasure

What else can I give away? Illusion of
submission. Halo of our dissonance,

please me. "Is" "power" "wrong" "?"
Pushing past the hold of pain, two animals

w/ faith in our excess,
excess that DGAF abt us but we harvest
every day.

Pay me with yr attention: our commerce in contact
Homage to interdependence, intertwin'd
transaction of veins rising & thy complement,
in whose likeness do I make thyself?

Yr teutonic overtones, blood in future's water
There's no more blood from me
unless u draw it *Quick lament for blood*
on the sheets Yr 1st time in the Pacific
& the water is oil slick trashed
and full of kelp heavy and plastered to
our nipples. *All eyes always 4 pleasure*

Smear of castor oil on wet skin
willingness to violate/be violated
apparent with every twitch, w/ every order
a supplication to becoming
Kneel down 4 me j once more

:If absence is constituted by presence, I
don't mind what we're fated to, white hot

embrace of abyss on the couch with its
pants around its ankles shoes still on and
u can take me hard now b/c in dreams
I speak your language:

want is fluent. From the 1st,
attending to speech like all good excesses
What is it to trod not upon each other

but side x side? What lubricates like *shush*?

Immanence of buckshot in thy flank,
barren woes about to get stuck all fertile
on your horns, galaxy of your disappearing
wrist j waiting to level the score

2 beasts tied up & suspended by a 3rd
floating like dying rose heads waiting
4 wind to blow us down to earth that's
yr fantasy u can explain it w
such lucidity it might have really
happened My fantasy is "real" it's the

Xtra sensory intelligence of desire
that knows yr presence before u enter
the room

alive in its perl, I have no skills
to offer but can splinter on
in oblivion for the memory
of undressing 4 yr lashes in the
porous night, butch er on the slab [my smolder er]

ROWAN POWELL

The ___ jumped over the __ (along a line a leap a landing)

I am writing to the history of Marie Germain, who in some year preceding the recording of the 'event' by Ambroise Paré in his 1573 text On Monsters and Marvels, ran, some way, along a path, chasing a pig, leaped a fence, and...

I am writing a letter, backwards, which they are telling me can only be sent forwards, the direction of travel from past to present, from cold to hot, from imperfect tending towards perfect. Onwards and upwards along the Great Chain of Being. In writing of Marie Germain, Ambroise Paré, who, without intention, wrote to me. To my body, running, wild in confusion. Paré states 'I do not write for women at all'. Across 446 years I write in reply, not to Paré, but to MG. I write to convey how little I can say, but how often I think and feel along that line, that leap and that landing. 1.68% T, twice daily. Sticky thing. I keep running, slipping through the thicket.Paré was a medical man, recording the facts as he saw them. A woman gives birth to a frog. Noted. Marie Germain runs too fast while chasing a pig, leaps and becomes a man. Record. This is simply cold tending towards its perfect opposite, heat. Paré is considered one of the fathers of surgery, repairing unwanted ruptures. A forerunner of modern forensic pathology, a pioneer in surgical techniques, he produced surgical advances in the treatment of wounds.

<u>Along</u>

Keeping pace means controlling breathing. Repeating on each foot strike to the ground; *a country of fences, stone walls, ditches and hedges*. Inhaling cold air, breathing out; *the quick, brown, fox, jumps, over, the lazy, dog.*

Through big belly trees who stretch out above. Wood for fuel. Wood for merchant ships and gun boats. Between 4–6,000 mature oaks—several hectares of forest—each ship. Each hectare is 100 meters square. A football field. A unit of measure. A play-space with all of its exclusion zones, white lines into grass.

Following what I imagine to be the closest approximation of your path, Marie, I search in the trees for a point of departure. I am looking for a suitable leap. Knowing that leaving the ground, with two feet, suspended, allows for an un-parting, two parts, at least two. Paré, Montaigne, and their boys, would say this is an improvement, the advancement towards a higher order, as nature tends towards perfection. *Fuck. That.* I exhale as I pace through the thicket, searching. Somewhere in history a leap, over a ditch. A fence, a hedge, a ditch, to hold me over. It's worth remembering that 'outlaw' was once used to refer to a 'wild' animal, especially an untameable horse. I am looking for this outlaw, a squealing sow, trotting obscenely away, willing to be chased. Back home I search online *can pigs run a 7 minute mile.* In a flash, the crossing. A gap, breached. Breached; to make a gap in and break through a wall, barrier, or defence. Of contract, to defy law. The possibility of an opening.

For now, I stand, held by the length of the divide.

A crackled YouTube video titled: *Austrian Woman Chasing A Pig.* This will help us get a sense of the scene. A pig bounding in a concrete courtyard. France? No, Austria. Close...ish. Two national border lines, 1,100km. It could be the '90s. There are two women, middle-age, wearing white aprons. The first woman calls out 'ARLOW' while the second ushers the pig from the corner of the screen. The pig trots obscenely from the right to the left of the screen. The farmhouse is now visible, a single story dark-wood clad building. Behind stands a well-manicured hedge providing a back fence to the farm scene. Around 4ft in height. Jumpable. The pig, now on the far left of the screen, reaches a smaller slatted fence with upright wooden panelling, with gaps in between. The weather is grey. No light cascades through the gaps. The pig now proceeds again to the right of the screen, and along the pavement, a car passes, a VW golf. I would date it around '93. Judging by the car, judging by the grain of the image. Judging by the women's faces. The pig is ushered again into the courtyard. Behind, green fields are visible, presumably for grazing cattle. Though fifth in the world, France ranks second in the EU in milk production, totaling 23.3 million metric tons a year. Not a bad haul. A global circuit of liquid sustenance, from body to bodies. *What did you want with that pig anyway?*

I stand, to one side, looking on, trying to squeeze the scene into being, wondering how my body has been rearranged. This is an attempt at *de la force de l'imagination.* For Montaigne, 'A strong imagination creates the event.' So here we have to set the scene, calculate the speeds, set everything in place, and then simple as the quick, brown, fox, jumps, over, the lazy, dog. Check hormones, a normal amount, healthy amounts, keep drinking. Regular levels. Nothing crossed. I think about practicing hurdle technique backwards by downloading the instructional video and running it in reverse. As I run in your image, I wonder how much of this chemical is porcine. Would that help? 1 billion pigs trotting around at any given time, squealing *chase me.*

While Paré is making his incisions, hundreds of little men build fences across Europe for little wages, cutting across open fields, villages, and common rights of access. Beady eyes peep through microscopes, increasingly obsessed with the precision of measuring instruments, squeezing value out. Countless incisions filled with granulation tissue to the level of the surrounding skin or new epithelium; no dead space, no avascular tissue; no signs or symptoms of infection; wound edges are open. Taxonomies of tissue.

Surgical instruments lined up like curios on a blue cloth background. From outside the edges of the screen, a pair of hands shuffle the objects around. Hands with no body, trimming the fat, putting the wild to work. Fences and ditches, winding like wound beds.

Paré wrote, before MG, Jeanne became Jean, from disporting and frolicking. Marie Pachea degenerated to Manuel. Fall. Back. Before them, still, in the same year the great King Frances made peace with the Swiss, a monster was born in Germany, having a head in the middle of its stomach; lived to be an adult; and the second smaller head took nourishment just like the other. Hungry little head. Notable yet no transgression.

Like a drop-pin, I place myself in the story, hungry and running, worrying about unwittingly slicing off bits of MG.

A line

Productivity is key, and pigs, unlike cows, cannot become pregnant while lactating. So pigs pose a severe economic problem to producers, a go-slow. While MG is running, greater efficiency in the collection of taxes by farmers enabled the French crown to gather a larger proportion of its revenue than ever before. This did not solve the problem of royal finance; the crown, in all of its luxury, still considered itself piss poor.

Breathing out to the rhythm of *England was to become a country of fences, stone walls, ditches and hedges.* Lines once drawn out sharp, become a blur again if you press your face close enough to the monitor, where they start to crackle and white becomes red, green, blue, millions of composite parts masquerading as continuity. 1000m: 2:30.70 National Record. Best in show. Prized.

The architecture of the wooden fence becomes ironic at the point that it is demonstrated that the limit of the woodland is defined by a recoded version of its own substance. Wood taken from woods to designate royal woodland. Copse like a corpse, a grotesque reconfiguration of itself, wood pulled from woods, bounding, defining its own absolute limit, both the crossing and the stopping. *England a country of fences, stone walls, ditches and hedges.* Again, having ruptured the ligaments by which they had been enclosed. *All I know is, I had a sow and Parliament took it away from me.*

Europe imagines itself for the first time as it clears its forests, running wood into paper mills and circulating its news back to itself. Following you following pig seems like a way through, to and from human form. Pig-oid, humanoid, porcine in porcelain. A hinney, molly, jack, jenny, jennet. Jumping back and forth mouth wide open, little hungry belly-mouth. A whole herd of feckless swine running across this wretched little land. I both want to make the jump and to collapse every contortion of my body-like-fence. To collapse sweetly with the pigs. Byron asked of the parliamentary attempts to contain and eradicate the radical movement of the Luddites: 'Can you commit a whole country to their own prisons?' This line of questioning is exhausting. God's little monsters. Draw the lines, cut it all up and we can deal with it later. Bleeding dry and squeezing.

In April 2018, the IAAF announced new 'differences of sex development' rules that required athletes with specific disorders of sex development, testosterone levels of 5 nmol/L and above, and certain androgen sensitivity, to take medication to lower their testosterone levels, effective beginning 8 May 2019. The narrow scope of the changes, which apply only to those athletes competing in the 400m, 800m, and 1500m implying that they whipped that one out specifically for Caster Semenya. New lines chalked down.

MG, I am thinking of an exact image, another to help us build this picture. It took a little while to find it, a couple of pages into the google search. The background in greens, long grass, the earth worn back to thick mud from the repeated trampling of feet. 12 individual pieces of sawn timber form a style. All but three planks run in the direction of the fence, while the remaining pieces form a small bench that intersects the fence at a right angle, providing enough elevation to step over the artificial boundary between what become two distinct fields, or plots of land, recognised and immortalised in covenants, contracts between two free individuals, two owners. The earth around the base of the crossing is claggy, the mud forms ridges where boots have recently stepped. The style is both awkward and elegant, static yet inviting motion. It is both the means of traversing the two physical spaces, and, in conjunction with the architecture of the fence, it provides the limit which marks out the spaces, the two fields now stand in opposition to each other. Private and distinct. Of their own and of their owners. I am thinking of you running, chasing an image of you, hybrid and porcine, wondering how to snap my back leg round hard enough to jolt an event. Crows clattering overhead, I wind through the thicket, I am looking for you, for a Jenny, for a Molly, a Jack, a Jennet, for some rogue chaotic animal.

Then we come to your trail leg, the secret to good hurdling technique. Just another even-toed ungulate. A big barrow, boar, feeder, squealing in delight, just out of my reach. CS called it; if you want to obliterate someone just tell them straight off. Don't creep around collecting data.

I lean into the screen where two electronically generated maps show a detail of Western Europe. Drawn as far east as to depict half of the Caspian Sea, and at the bottom of the image the north of Africa is visible although the data-set demonstrating the density of forest coverage does not extend to Egypt or Algeria. All but the tips of these countries are left white indicating no data. The darkest green area illustrates the densest forest, the red is the least. Trees thinning. Change over time illustrated from an impossible no-where space. Middle-distance. 800 meters. Height, 5ft 10 inches. Weight 154lbs. It seems plausible, with this physiognomy.

For a better sense of the correct method it is important to consult experts. It will no longer do to listen to the body alone. A tall athletic man relays instructions while standing next to an 8 foot wired fence. The hurdle is placed against the fence and the man repeatedly raises his lead leg smashing it against the metal lattice which tremors in reply. This is the action of the trail leg.

A leap
Tresspasser. A high stone wall. I continue to obsessively study 'improving your hurdle technique' online, the red curve of the track guiding from the right to the left of the image as drills, mini disciplines, are suggested. Over and over. I was young when I heard recounted to me the terror and excitement of being chased off farmland, thinking there was a gun, scaling over to escape with superhuman force. Even then I wanted to be part of the chase. At such a point for MG, Paré recorded 'the male rod came to be developed in him, having ruptured the ligaments by which they had been enclosed.'

As I run, I repeat to myself: the key components to hurdling are your ability to run over the hurdles. Not to prepare for them, be in a full sprint, and literally take them as you take the race. *The impossibility of not imagining*. Crucial technical parts are your lead leg, which is the first leg to go over the hurdle. Now you take this out in front of you and snap down as quickly as you can in a semi-straight position. Then we come to your trail leg. This is the last leg to go over the hurdle and you need to pull it round as fast as you can, leading with the knee, driving the foot through to run off the hurdle as fast as you can. The arm motion is a snap, you really bring your arm forward with the lead leg and snap it back so you can go straight back into your stride and rhythm.

Silence came after the landing. Two feet, back on the soft dirt after the ditch. Something changed or nothing. Or maybe this wasn't even an event until it came to be retold, imbued with significance after the fact. MG leapt, degenerated, while chasing an escaped pig. So in fact it was language that came after the landing, not silence. The event degenerated. It was narration and meaning, and only then signification. Otherwise there was just a leap. So only now, after Paré, after Montaigne, after every other inscription over and on top of a running jump, after this, and every other retelling, after the song, a warning, and after the landing.

An imagined synchronised leap, degenerate security. A moment of instantaneous collective accord, the snap, the imagined collective 'yes' that birthed the Hobbsean sovereign body politik, the great Leviathan, securer, protector. Another leap. Contractual individual mastery and ownership of alienable property, unimagined. Or, instead, a collective leap, up at once, the collapse of all fences and all ditches filled, levelled.

No more. That's. My. pig. That's. My. wood. You dropped it. I picked it up. 400 meters. Running.

A landing

History bifurcating, we run fingers along the furrows we now inhabit. Two gigantic intellectual traditions formed from the simple act of picking up wood. Subsistence turned theft. One the one hand, Marx's critique of capitalism, on the other, criminology. Hands on. Hands off.

No Freud, no DNA, without anatomy, dissection, clinician. We can imagine that for the Renaissance mind a static immutable body didn't register. But still, now, then, bodies, my body do not flow. Cut, a line, an incision. Marking out one side from the other. A stitch, a gate with a step, knotting two halves back as one. Paré was a surgeon.

In June 2019 the Swiss Supreme Court temporarily suspended the IAAF rule that requires all DSD athletes to reduce their testosterone to below five nmol/L for at least six months if they want to compete internationally at all distances from 400m to a mile.

Silence came after the landing. Then the chatter of historians, clamouring at the gate. Archeologists in the ditches. Small items dusted with small brushes. The nails from the fence, each, one, bagged, numbered, catalogued and registered. We are really making some progress here.

The International Association of Athletics Federation's policy on hyperandrogenism, or high natural levels of testosterone in women, was suspended following the case of Dutee Chand v. Athletics Federation of India (AFI) & The IA AAF, in the Court of Arbitration for Sport, decided in July 2015. The ruling found that there was a lack of evidence provided that testosterone increased female athletic performance and notified the IAAF that it had two years to provide the evidence, to stay within the lines.

Imagine England in 1688, twenty million acres of it pasture, meadow, forest, heath moor mountain. That's a quarter of the whole thing. You'd have to do some running to find your hurdle.

Such rights are separately defined in each case. Ancient rights of common were usually of five kinds:
Rights of pasture: the right to graze livestock; sheep, horses, cattle, pigs.
Right of estovers: the right to cut and take wood (but not timber), reeds, heather, bracken.
Right of turbary: the right to dig turf or peat for fuel.
Right in the soil: the right to take sand, gravel, stone, coal, minerals.
Right of piscary: the right to take fish from ponds, streams.
Right leg goes first. The strong leg. The correct leg. Silence came after the landing.
Two feet, back on the soft dirt after the ditch. Something changed or nothing.
Having ruptured the ligaments by which they had been enclosed.
Splitting-two-worlds. Chasing pig.

The girls of that place have, to this day, a song, wherein they advise one another not to take too great strides.

A line.
A leap.
A landing.

400 meters.
800 meters.
1500 meters.

Oestrogen levels. Testosterone levels. Regulated. I run along the edges of these images, stitching them clumsily together. Looking back to a Europe yet to imagine itself, to draw itself out. I run until I can't. Collapsing me onto Marie onto Manuel, onto Jeanne, onto Jean, onto MG, onto Paré, CS, the surgeon, DC, my body, wild in confusion, a sow, this animal. Glorious.

SAMUEL ACE

Every morning I wait for a pouch of dreams

Every morning I wait for a pouch of dreams   the scrabblings of birds and all the rushings by   my parents call from two different corners of the room   suddenly dead martyrs in the stories of their recent lives   my mother lives in a new house   she tells me she loves the windows that look out to the sea   she shows me her kitchen   far messier than the one she had before   my father   singing and bald at twenty-five shovels dirt or coal   I hum along with him but I'm not sure he hears   I ask my mother if she's seen my sisters   Who? she shouts   all the hairs!   all the mouths!   she does not know the tall rangy man in overalls   gone before she recognizes him   my father walking down a path near the river   where the after-life happens before it can be caught   where the life before is a dog or a fly or a portrait on the wall   my sisters stroll through the center of the room   one has a broken arm   the other a cane and a limp   I run to them and hide beneath their matching rose velvet gowns   I sing my father's song up through their ribs and hear an orchestra of breathing tubes   rabbits on the floor   a hint of lime   eggs scrambling in an iron pan   I see a block of marble where the wind   a drum in the grass   a grave of killers who rise and wander toward morning through the dark

Then there is the penis the warehouse farm where the penis grows inside the penis room next to hands blooming in the hand room hearts budding in the heart room ears flowering in the ear room the whole-baby room stands adjacent to the brain room at the end of the hall it's now so simple to create a brain at the end of the hall the most primitive machine of all in a rare occurrence just last week an intact human was found hiding in an oil barrel on the banks of the Cuyahoga half-buried in neon-green muck captured only after an honest bounty was paid *please* the human said *please* their face strangely congruent under the searchlights and ant-like drones shining past jeep tracks in the sand up against the concrete walls painted green with cheery dogs

Blood yes

Blood yes I'm thinking not of sacrifice and bargains but of eating my own retch I have been in the stocks and on the racks I have asked to be taken asked to succumb I have been the flanagan women been of men and motors a servant and subject of pain of scrawls in doorways that open to gravel-smelling worlds with vats of hot tar and the hand of a good foreman I have been the child in a family of predators the submissive of a fraternity boy I have stumbled grandiose into gardens full of enlightenment and shame unable to void or step safely onto the sand I have expected something more than food pushed through grates something more than human the small of me flung off carpets at the entrance of a smoke-filled home

I hear a dog who is always in my death

How is it you bring me back to the cliffs   the bright heads of eagles   the vessels of grief in the soil?   I dig for you with a gentle bit of lighter fluid and three miniature rakes   burning only a single speck of dirt to touch a twig as tiny as a neuron   or even smaller   one magic synapse inside the terminus limbs of your breath

The fighter jets fly over the house every hour   no sound but inside our hands   I hear a far chime and I am cold   a north wind and the grit of night   first the murmur then the corpse   first the paddling then the banquet   first the muzzle then the hanging the plea   first the break then the tap the tap   I hear your skin   the reach of your arms the slick along your thighs   more floorboard than step   first the flannel then the gag first the bells   then the exhale

I hear a dog who is always in my death   the breath of a mother who holds a gun   a pillow in the shape of a heart   first the planes then the criminal ponds   first the ghost boats then the trains   first the gates then the bargain   a child formed from my fingertip and the eye of my grandmother's mother   a child born at 90   the rise and rush of air   a child who walks from the gas

These Nights

I've left the door open to the vision coming through the dark   his arms filter through the flowered ceiling   unsealed from the jeweled tree in the window   his organ hurtles through the air into the pond   where I search for a mirror and some softer chalk   a surface so pliable   so dug and raw   that the baby's breathy touch   the wind   some creosote so faint   begs the otter to swim   on this   my first and last day

But it's early morning in someone else's house   out the window a New England dawn   mist on the green and turquoise bed   the pound of feet upstairs   then a rush of cold air   a walk down the stairs   a winter relationship or a pact of privacy before the lights come on   what's left is the result of criminals   the orange a rendering some thready hope that the white man lost   but he did not lose

Could it not it be night again?   a boy   his beard   his hat the only orange intact inside our bed   our hold heading down as if it were a normal day   when our viewing habits were not caught public on the street   how did they know?   did I somehow tip them off?   first they took my sweater   then the card with his name   when stumbling they marched us down the long-halled building to a cell   the blood fountain   where soon I even lost the ocean smell of wind in the after-rot rushing from the open doors of trains

STEPHEN IRA

from An Elizabeth

an adaptation of Mario Martino's Emergence

"But I felt: you are an *I*
you are an *Elizabeth*
you are one of *them.*
Why should you be one, too?"

Elizabeth Bishop
"In the Waiting Room"

Sometimes Elizabeth sent Elizabeth to discipline me and his words were sharp, not to be disobeyed. Perhaps this is what whetted my appetite for what came later. Once, and just once, he hit me under the chin and I almost bit my tongue in half, not only from the force but from the surprise of it. It brought the first real joy: that order could surprise. Against Elizabeth's orders I'd run off alone to the park, and Elizabeth was within his rights in punishing me. I trod the well-laid paths, read the historical material and statue plaques: *Elizabeth, Elizabeth, Elizabeth*...I loved him, worshipped him, and forgave him all at the same time. I found new orders in the animals at the back of our house—the ants and diffuse squirrels—and I sought that jolt through study, too. When Elizabeth joined the institution and went away, the house seemed empty. I discovered in the esoterica of books like *Robert's Rules* scenarios that made the thrill of sudden strikes seem workaday. When Elizabeth sent me his old Army hat I folded and tucked it in the pocket of his hand-me-down shirts and this gave me a feeling of comrade-spirit with all men in uniform. I felt I knew their names and they knew mine. I'd join their ranks as soon as I grew up.

Applicant Elizabeth

In early February I applied for entrance into the Order of St. Elizabeth and was accepted. I had heard of rejections, of course, or girls who simply didn't take to contact lenses or similar, but not many. To provide my dowry ($300) and required wardrobe, I left school and worked at two jobs: nurses aide at two hospitals, one Elizabethan, one secular. I liked the work, and each time I learned more, the thrill of the I that had been there went through me. Of course I wrote Elizabeth and Elizabeth about my decision, and for some reason Elizabeth expressed neither pleasure nor displeasure. He enclosed perfunctory mementos of his starch-collared schoolboy days. Unnatural for him. As much as it was custom. Was he afraid of a second failure? Wasn't it true that all customs were natural to him, and had I inherited this form of pleasure? On the first day of May I entered the novitiate, Elizabeth on the River. Twenty-two carven steps up that embankment, and twenty-two bad false marble falls down. My welcome was jubilant, with excited postulants and novices, even the Mistress of Novices, Sister Elizabeth, crowding round me. My newness became our general awe of the place: the rock hard mountain of black mud as bright as glass, cut through with stairs to comb the clouds of mist, and shrouded in more mist up at its top, the brutalist institution. It was with a new kind of exhilaration that I entered the little curtained room, which was to be my cell for the next two and a half years. I had no little window to see that view from the inside. My new black dress covered me down to the tips of my black shoes, the sleeves stopped just short of my wrists. I would never have chosen it, nor any of the clothing I had ever seen. A stiff white collar was attached at the neck of the black cape which extended the length of the forearm. Giggling, all assured me I would feel the tendrils of my collar creeping up soon to my mouth—and then I did. Sister Elizabeth now placed a black veil with white trim around my head, leaving only the front hair visible.

Acrobat Elizabeth

"Why are you staring at the floors?" Elizabeth asked. I was wondering what they were made of and how they had been shipped to the white rooms of this mountain. "I was wondering if they are easy to clean." Upon that point, the material would matter less, I realized, than the sheer amount. "It all depends on how you look at it." She looked intrigued by me. She looked resigned. "If you don't mind the process—the whole thing, that is—you won't mind. If you don't mind the acrobatics of polishing and waxing—well, who knows? Strangely enough, ambition can indeed carry a person here. One girl actually thinks it's fun." If you wanted clean whites then why lay a white floor? "Well, bully for her!" I declared, as she looked at me. She looked at me, almost suspiciously, and then a grin of appreciation spread over her small impish face. "Elizabeth!" she breathed. "Careful!" she warned. And oh, I knew that I wasn't an Elizabeth like her. "How's it done?" I wanted to know. "Like so." I wanted something to hate. She obliged by demonstrating. I watched. "You put a soft cloth under your feet, then slide back and forth." I slid back and forth. "Inch by inch." After just a few iterations I felt myself forget to do it and so keep going. I wanted to laugh for the first time that day.

Thinning Elizabeth

After dinner I was given my assignment for the week: laundry work. I dreamed of bleach thinning my fingers out before I could dilute it. Then I helped with the dishes before going back to the dorm to unpack and talk with the girls. One said, "You go on dreaming just like that and they will love you for it." I learned that homework was not to begin until the opening of the school term and that was still two weeks away. I resolved I would devote myself to kinds of dreams that fueled the mountain's crown. There was ample time for playing girl's games or watching TV. And sure, these deep creep into dreams, but I could not tell whether they were meant to: the rack and the screw, the bell book and candle, Red Rover, and on a high brown note the installation table set with genital dinners for all the Elizabeths. Personal warmth appeared nonexistent. Perhaps it had to pass from regiment to regiment. Some kids had brothers and sisters here, but for the most part, we were lone individuals who came from all over the diocese. I didn't like it. I was being regimented and I didn't like it. Every little shake gave the jolt; that was new and too much. Still, it was better than the kind of fighting going on at home. I was developing a set of values but I would still need to understand them once they were done, so something would have to be left. On the third day I received a letter from Elizabeth, in which she'd enclosed a picture of Elizabeth's wedding. They all looked so fine in their smocks with the educational lettering. It was the first time I'd seen a picture of Elizabeth, the girl he'd married. I asked myself, how does Elizabeth smile? She was smiling as brides do, and long brown hair curled around her small, sweetheart face. "Swathed in gauze," as the poet says, she had gone so far in you could barely see her eyes. Elizabeth was exactly the kind of girl I'd marry!

He was so unrehearsed, just that well trained. So warm and kind. Just a "great mind," although he would never say so. My ideal woman. How the thinning of the fingers might reward one. How lucky Elizabeth was. How her sophistication now followed even into photographs, as would an expression of great pain. How lucky Elizabeth always was. How foolish to forget what drew me here. I was on kitchen duty the second week and, accidentally, one of the kids spilled scalding milk down my legs.

Jolted Elizabeth

From that first glance I'd disliked the institutional look of the place, and, once inside, even the many pictures of saints did nothing to change my opinion. Not even the life size oil painting of the Philosopher, not all the way. Not even the life size oil painting of the Bishop. I wanted what they offered, but I wasn't what they promised on the other end and suddenly I didn't know how that might change. This just wasn't where I wanted to be. And there was the jolt: desire in the white room, thrown against the bookshelf where the paperbacks are sparse—audible, too. I had the sudden impulse to bolt and run away. Equally as strong, the pull to find what more I could object to here, run then. But to run would solve nothing. Even if my body became one of theirs, I would walk in it. I had to graduate to make money to go to Denmark.

SYLVIA RIVERA

BITCH ON WHEELS: A Speech by Sylvia Rivera, June 2001

We did have connections with the Mafia. You must remember, everyone was doing drugs back then. Everyone was selling drugs, and everybody was buying drugs to take to other bars, like myself. I was no angel. I would pick up my drugs at the Stonewall and take them to the Washington Square Bar on 3rd Street and Broadway, which was the drag queen third world bar. Even back then we had our racist little clubs. There were the white gay bars and then there were the very few third world bars and drag queen bars.

The night of the Stonewall, it happened to be the week that Judy Garland had committed suicide. Some people say that the riots started because of Judy Garland's death. That's a myth. We were all involved in different struggles, including myself and many other transgender people. But in these struggles, in the Civil Rights movement, in the war movement, in the women's movement, we were still outcasts. The only reason they tolerated the transgender community in some of these movements was because we were gung-ho, we were front liners. We didn't take no shit from nobody. We had nothing to lose. *You* all had rights. We had nothing to lose. I'll be the first one to step on any organization, any politician's toes if I have to, to get the rights for my community.

Back to the story: we were all in the bar, having a good time. Lights flashed on, we knew what was coming; it's a raid. This is the second time in one week that the bar was raided. Common practice says the police from the 6th Precinct would come in to each gay bar and collect their payoff. Routine was, "Faggots over here, dykes over here, freaks over there," referring to my side of the community. If you did not have three pieces of male attire on you, you were going to jail. Just like a butch dyke would have to have three pieces of female clothing, or *he* was going to jail. The night goes on, you know, they proof you for ID, you know, back then you could get away with anything. Fake IDs were great back then, because I wasn't even 18 yet; I was gonna turn 18. We are led out of the bar. The routine was that the cops get their payoff, they confiscate the liquor, if you were a bartender you would snatch the money as soon as the lights went on because you would never see that money again. A padlock would go on the door. What we did, back then, was disappear to a coffee shop or any place in the neighborhood for fifteen minutes. You come back, the Mafia was there cutting the padlock off, bringing in more liquor, and back to business as usual.

Well, it just so happened that that night it was muggy; everybody was being, I guess, cranky; a lot of us were involved in different struggles; and instead of dispersing, we went across the street. Part of history forgets, that as the cops are inside the bar, the confrontation started outside by throwing change at the police. We started with the pennies, the nickels, the quarters, and the dimes. "Here's your payoff, you pigs! You fucking pigs! Get out of our faces." This was started by the street queens of that era, which I was part of, Marsha P. Johnson, and many others that are not here. I'm lucky to by 50 in July, but I'm still here, and I'll be damned if I won't see 100.

One thing led to another. The confrontation got so hot, that Inspector Pine, who headed this raid, him and his men had to barricade themselves in our bar, because they could not get out. The people that they had arrested, they had to take into the bar with them, because there was no police backup for them. But seriously, as history tells it, to this day, we don't know who cut the phone lines! So they could not get the call to the 6th precinct. Number one, Inspector Pine was not welcome in the 6th precinct because he had just been appointed to stop the corruption and, you know, what they called back then, we were a bunch of deviants, perverts. So he was there for that purpose, so who knows if one of his own men didn't do it, that was, you know, taking a payoff himself.

The police and the people that were arrested were barricaded inside this bar, with a *Village Voice* reporter, who proceeded to tell his story, in the paper, that he was handed a gun. The cops were actually so afraid of us that night that if we had busted through the bar's door, they were gonna shoot. They were ordered to shoot if that door busted open. Someone yanked a parking meter out of the ground. It was loose, you know, I don't know how it got loose. But that was being rammed into the door.

People have also asked me, "Was it a pre-planned riot?," because out of nowhere, Molotov cocktails showed up. I have been given the credit for throwing the first Molotov cocktail by many historians but I always like to correct it; I threw the second one, I did not throw the first one! And I didn't even know what a Molotov cocktail was; I'm holding this thing that's lit and I'm like "What the hell am I supposed to do with this?" "Throw it before it blows!" "OK!"

The riot did get out of hand, because there was Cookie's down the street, there was The Haven, there was the Christopher's End. Once word of mouth got around that the Stonewall had gotten raided, and that there's a confrontation going on, people came from the clubs. But we also have to remember one thing: that it was not just the gay community and the street queens that really escalated this riot; it was also the help of the many radical straight men and women that lived in the Village at the time, that knew the struggle of the gay community and the trans community.

So the crowds did swell. You know, it was a long night of riots. It was actually very exciting cause I remember howling all through the streets, "The revolution is here!", you know? Cars are being turned over, windows are being broken, fires are being set all over the place. Blood was shed. When the cops did finally get there, the reinforcements, forty five minutes later, you had the chorus line of street queens kicking up their heels, singing their famous little anthem that up to today still lives on: "We are the Stonewall girls/ we wear our hair in curls/ we wear our dungarees/ above our nelly knees/ we show our pubic hairs," and so on and so forth.

At the time, there were many demonstrations. They were fierce demonstrations back then. I don't know how many people remember those times, or how many people read of the struggle in this whole country, what was going on. So then the tactical police force came and heads were being bashed left and right. But what I found very impressive that evening, was that the more that they beat us, the more we went back for. We were determined that evening that we were going to be a liberated, free community, which we did acquire that. Actually, I'll change the 'we': *You* have acquired your liberation, your freedom, from that night: Myself: I've got shit, just like I had back then. But I still struggle, I still continue the struggle. I will struggle til the day I die and my main struggle right now is that my community will seek the rights that are justly ours.

I am tired of seeing my children—I call everything including yous in this room, you are all my children—I am tired of seeing homeless transgender children; young, gay, youth children. I am tired of seeing the lack of interest that this rich community has. This is a very affluent community. When we can afford to re-renovate a building for millions and millions of dollars and buy another building across the street and still not worry about your homeless children from your community, and I know this for a fact, because the reason I have to get clearance every time to come into this building is because I saw many of the kids before the building was renovated up the street, many of the children are sleeping on the steps of that church. I went in there with an attitude. I raised hell. Yes, maybe I did try to destroy the front desk, but I did not attack anybody. But what did this community center do to me? My thanks for everything I have done for this freakin' community? Had me arrested and put in Bellevue! So I'm supposed to kiss their asses? No, I don't kiss nobody's ass cause I haven't lived this long, because I don't kiss nobody's ass.

That night, I remember singing "We Shall Overcome," many a times, on different demonstrations, on the steps of Albany, when we had our first march, when I spoke to the crowds in Albany. I remember singing but I haven't overcome a damn thing. I'm not even in the back of the bus. My community is being pulled by a rope around our neck by the bumper of the damn bus that stays in the front. Gay liberation but transgender nothing! Yes, I hold a lot of anger. But I have that right. I have that right to have that anger. I have fought too damn hard for this community to put up with the disrespect that I have received and my community has received for the last thirty-two years.

And a point of history, you know that it took the Gay Rights Bill here in New York seventeen years to pass. But I'll go through the beginning. When we were petitioning for the Gay Rights Bill, there was only one person that was arrested. That was me. Because I had the guts to go into the Times Square area on 42nd Street and petition the people to sign that petition. And the only reason I did it was because that bill did include the transgender community. Two or three years into the movement and the bill is being presented and we're going back and forth to City Hall. They have a little backroom deal without inviting Miss Sylvia and some of the other trans activists to this backroom deal with these politicians. The deal was, "You take them out, we'll pass the bill." So, what did nice conservative gay white men do? They sell a community that liberated them down the river, and it still took them seventeen years to get the damn bill passed! And I hate to say it, but I was very happy. Every time that that bill came up for a vote, I said, "I hope it doesn't pass," because of what they did to me. As badly as I knew this community needed that bill, I didn't feel it was justified for them to have it on my sweat and tears, or from my back.

So Stonewall is a great, great foundation. It began the modern day liberation movement, like we spoke before about the Daughters of Bilitis and the Mattachine Society. Yes, there were lots of other little groups but you had to be what they called themselves the "normal homosexuals." They wore suits and ties. One of the first demonstrations that they had, lesbians who'd never even worn dresses were wearing dresses and high heels to show the world that they were normal. Normal? Fine.

One of my best friends now, who has employed me for the last seven years before I changed jobs, is Randy Wicker. Randy Wicker was a very well-known gay male activist in 1963. He was the first gay male - before any real movement was there - to get on a talk show and state to the world that he was a *normal* homosexual. I give him credit for that. He has done a lot of different things, but he also in 1969 and for many years trashed the transgender community. It took him a lot of years to wake up and realize that we are no different than anybody else; that we bleed, that we cry, and that we suffer.

But this has been going on for the longest time. I mean, before gay liberation, it was the same thing: "drag queens over there; we're over here." The world came tumbling down in 1969 and on the fourth anniversary of the Stonewall movement, of the Stonewall riot, the transgender community was silenced because of a radical lesbian named Jean O'Leary, who felt that the transgender community was offensive to women because we liked to wear makeup and we liked to wear miniskirts. Excuse me! It goes with the business that we're in at that time! Because people fail to realize that - not trying to get off the story - everybody thinks that we want to be out on them street corners. No we do not. We don't want to be out there sucking dick and getting fucked up the ass. But that's the only alternative that we have to survive because the laws do not give us the right to go and get a job the way we feel comfortable. I do not want to go to work looking like a man when I know I am not a man. I have been this way since before I left home and I have been on my own since the age of ten.

Anyway, Jean O'Leary started the big commotion at this rally. It was the year that Bette Midler performed for us. I was supposed to be a featured speaker that day. But being that the women felt that we were offensive, the drag queens Tiffany and Billy were not allowed to perform. I had to fight my way up on that stage and literally, people that I called my comrades in the movement, literally beat the shit out of me. That's where it all began, to really silence us. They beat me, I kicked their asses. I did get to speak, I got my points across.

There was another speaker that day, Lee Brewster (she passed a year ago), very well known to the trans community and to the cross dressing community. She got up on stage, threw her tiara to the crowd and said, "Fuck gay liberation." But what people fail to realize was that Lee Brewster put up a majority of the money for the Gay Pride March of 1970, which was our first one. And it was once again, out of maybe two or three hundred of us that started from the Village, up 6th Avenue, up two little lanes of traffic, that we were the visible ones. We were the visible ones, the trans community. And still and yet, if you notice where they keep pushing us every year, we're further and further towards the back. I have yet to have the pleasure to march with my community, for the simple fact that I belong to the Stonewall Live Veterans group, I march in the front.

But until my community is allowed the respect to march in the front, I will go march with my community because that's where I'm needed and that's where I belong. And yes, I'll wear my big sash that says "Stonewall." And people are gonna ask. And I'm gonna tell why; because this is where the Heritage of Pride wants to keep us. You see, I don't pull no punches, I'm not afraid to call out no names. You screw with the transgender community and the organization Street Transgender Action Revolutionaries will be on your doorstep. Just like we trashed the HRC for not endorsing the Amanda Milan actions, and then when they threw us a piece of trash, we refused to accept it. How dare you question the validity of a transgender group asking for your support, when this transgender woman was murdered? No. The trans community has allowed, we have allowed the gay and lesbian community to speak for us. Times are changing. Our armies are rising and we are getting stronger. And when we come a knocking (that includes from here to Albany to Washington) they're going to know that you don't fuck with the transgender community.

Mainstreaming, normality, being normal. I understand how much everybody likes to fit into that mainstream gay and lesbian community. You know, it used to be a wonderful thing to be avant-garde, to be different from the world. I see us reverting into a so-called liberated closet because we, not we, *yous* of this mainstream community, wish to be married, wish for this status. That's all fine. But you are forgetting your grass roots, you are forgetting your own individual identity. I mean, you can never be *like them*. Yes we can adopt children, all well and good, that's fine. I would love to have children. I would love to marry my lover over there, but for political reasons I will not do it because I don't feel that I have to fit into that closet of normal, straight society which the gay mainstream is always going towards.

This is why they don't want the transgender people to have rights. This is why they always tell us, "Oh let us get ours, and then we'll help you get yours." If I hear that one more time, I think I'll jump off the Empire State building. But I'm sure a lot of people would like that, especially the old-timers, because I have actually mellowed down through the years. I used to be a bitch on wheels.

But these are days that we have to reflect on. This is a month that's very important. I may have a lot of anger but it means a lot to me because after being at World Pride last year in Italy, to see 500,000 beautiful, liberated gay men, women, and trans people and being called the mother of the world's transgender movement and gay liberation movement, it gives me great pride to see my children celebrating. But I just hope that - and I've heard a lot of positive things in this room tonight, as far as people realizing that the trans community was your benefactor and that people are opening up their eyes. But you got to remember, don't just say that because we're here; show your support when we send out a call for action to support our actions, the things that we plan to do.

I mean, it was a hurting feeling that on May 4th, 2001 we had history-breaking civil rights in for city council. Our bill was finally introduced. Wow! We waited this long! But where were my sisters and brothers? Where were my children that I liberated? Very few allies showed up. But what made me proud was that the trans community showed up in numbers, and the girls that work these corners even got the nerve enough to come into public and go onto something that they would never consider doing, which was to walk on City Hall because they are all afraid of the police, but they were there. So, that goes to show the rest of the community, that technically when we ask for your support, we want your support. But in the long run, if it's not there, we will acquire what we need.

But, we must remember: Amanda Milan's actions are coming up. I hope to see a lot of you there. But remember one thing, when you fell out en masse, including myself, for Matthew Shepard, and many of us went to jail, I only got to see maybe five minutes of the whole thing because being the person who I am, a front liner, as soon as I sat down in the street, one of the white shirts that has known me for years, the person says, "When the order goes down, get that bitch right there, get her off the street and into the paddy wagon." So that's the way that went.

But it seemed like everybody and their mother came out for Matthew Shepard. A white, middle class gay boy that was effeminate! Amanda Milan got killed last year, five days before Gay Pride. We waited a month to have a vigil for her. Three hundred people showed up. What kind of a - doesn't the community have feelings? We are part of the gay and lesbian community! That really hurt me, to see that only three hundred people showed up. And it's not like it was gonna be a long vigil, I mean we went from 36th Street to 42nd Street. So, when we call people, not only to sponsor our actions, we expect to see bodies there. I mean, but like I said, we're capable of doing it on our own because that's what we're learning now, after thirty-two years, that we cannot depend on nobody, except our own trans community, to keep pushing forward.

But remember that as you celebrate this whole month, of how you are liberated. And I feel so sorry for those that are not able to read the history of the Stonewall around the world. And we have to blame once again all the publishers and whatnot. I tried to push Martin Duberman's publishers to have the Stonewall book translated into Spanish. But they felt that the book would not sell in Third World countries, in Latin countries. Which is a lot of crap! Because the only way that you're going to learn the history, especially if you're far away and just coming out, is to be able to pick up a book and read about the history of the Stonewall and how you were liberated. I know many of our countries are not as liberated as the United States, as far as the gays are concerned, especially Latin American countries, because once again you got to remember that we have to play that big macho role, you know, men, we have to make lots of babies! But it's a shame that it has taken thirty-two years for people to finally realize how much we have given to you, to realize the history of the trans involvement in this movement. And in that note, I hope to see yous when I send out the emails to you, and I hope you pass that on. That I hope to see a lot of yous there for the Amanda Milan actions and I once again wish yous all a very happy gay pride day but also think about us.

T FLEISCHMANN

from Time Is the Thing a Body Moves Through

By the medieval era, several places had been reached, each
named Thule, and each determined to not, in fact, be Thule.
Cartographers began to indicate ultima Thule to clarify this.
This ultima was the Thule that had not been ddiscovered, the
Thule that explorers hadn't reached and that needed to be
distinguished from the Thules they had found and that they
still wanted to write on the map.
The Thules and Thilas and Thulas of the frozen coasts—
real places with bearded men and dinners of fish and fermented liquids—
their names mark them as less, their movement from the exal-
tation of what could be and into the tired reality of what is.
Simon explains this all to me as we lie in bed, having
woken early and at the same time.
He returned last night from Maine, visiting a gay bar where
the men had salt on their faces while I stayed behind, reading
and smoking cigarettes on his roof.
These are some of my favorite moments, when one of us
has gone somewhere else, and then we come back to each
other.
I close my eyes, thinking I might fall back asleep soon, and
letting Simon's voice fill the map of my imagination while
I do.

That billboard of the unmade bed, those two pillow dimples from two heads—
an installation at Brighton Beach, Berlin, Paris.
Spotlights on a corner,
as any two people in love might be.

In 1990, walking around Los Angeles, Felix Gonzales-Torres and Ross came upon *Gold Field* in a gallery.
A work by Roni Horn, it is a rectangle of forty-nine by sixty inches, two pounds of pure gold pressed so thin that it rises barely above one-hundredth of a millimeter.
Horn's intention with the piece was to allow viewers to appreciate and respond to the gold absent the economic, political, and social histories that suffuse the material.
Knowing that Ross was approaching death, the couple came across the flat gold, and, in the artist's words,
"There it was, in a whie room, all by itself, it didn't need company, it didn't need anything.
Sitting on the floor, ever so lightly.
A new landscape, a possible horizon, a place of rest and absolute beauty....
Ross and I were lifted.
That gesture was all we needed to rest, to think about the possibility of change.
This showed the innate ability of an artist proposing to make this place a better place.
How truly revolutionary."
The revolutionary potential in Horn's flat gold is not in contrast to her desire to extract the metal from those political histories,
but rather it is an accomplice to it, a transcendence.
Where the gold sends you, I think,
is to a better version of the world you are in,
with a golden light to it.

Gonzalez-Torres and Ross continued, briefly, to live in Los Angeles,
the city being the only place they cohabited, with Ross dying about six months later.
After encountering the piece, they called every sunset they say "the Gold Field,"
Horn having, as Gonzalez-Torres said,
"named something that had always been there."

Simon and I, hiking back from the waterfall, commit to visit Iceland and Greenland together.
He will take photographs of the ice, and I will write of it,
we decide, although how we think we will pay for this trip, we don't say.
"You need that space, you need that lifting up, you need that traveling in your mind that love brings, transgressing the limits of your body and your imagination,"
Gonzalez-Torres said, explaining the import of love to art.
Which is true, although it is not clear to me, what it is that I am imagining Simon and I are together, when I am imagining we are together,
somewhere else.
I say,
"You know that I'm talking about you when I talk about the ice,"
and he assures me that he understands, which I accept,
although this is the most directly we have spoken of ourselves to date.
On this hike, we often must decide if we will step on a thin sheet of ice, which might break and release us into the cold and shallow creek water,
or slip across the ice-slicked shale and limestone.
Sometimes Simon reaches out and grabs my arm, so I don't fall,
and when one of us does slip, we each break into laughter,

happy with the sun shining gray, or maybe silver, thorugh the
bare branches of the trees.

But no matter how far away you manage to get, still you will
find yourself there.
The northernmost base of the United States Air Force is the
Thule Air Base, in Greenland, 750 miles north of the Arctic
Circle's boundary,
its location decided by the U.S. and the Kingdom of Denmark.
Its closest neighboring village, across sixty-five miles of ice
and stone, is Qaanaaq,
home to the Inughuit population who were forcibly displaced
north when the base came;
in 1951, a group of hunters returned from an expedition to
find the American military there, raising buildings and pre-
paring for a potential nuclear escalation in the Korean war.
The Thule Air Base today fulfills a few functions, primarily
keeping watch for (and potentially shooting down) inter-
continental ballistic missles headed to the Unied States,
its location being halfway between Moscow and Washington,
while assisting with the Global Positioning System, perform-
ing satellite surveillance, and housing advanced weapons,
among whatever other secrets conspire there.
It is where, in 1968, a subsonic bomber crashed into ice, dam-
aging and nearly detonating four hyrogen bombs.
One bomb was lost forever, its twelve kilograms of plutonium
dispersed in the ecosystem, where furless seals now sometimes
roll on the glaciers
What a pair—
that imagined perfect ice, so much of it that Simon's imagistic
obsession and mine, twinned, might be unitd there,
and our militarized state, with its enduring aggressions, ensur-
ing that the ice will melt.
This is not a Thule imagined, not the place Christopher

Columbus claimed to have seen, but one made,
built on ruins over six centuries old, as soldiers communicate
with far-flung satellites and missiles.
It's a place that is often accessible only by aircraft, where not
a single road leads.
It's on a map, so even if you can't go there, still, you can
find it.

Is beauty panacean, able always to instill in us moments of
transcendence?
Or does the sun just melt the ice,
beauty appreciated only when it is the constituent hum of a
thing that fades?

"When people ask me,
'Who is your public?'
I say honestly, without skipping a beat,
'Ross.'
The public was Ross,"
Gonzalez-Torres asserted.
And really, no matter how public the art, the speech act,
no matter how many people are gathered around the table, aren't
we at our core just speaking to one person?
If today I spoke with one person,
and if we both heard one another,
there might be enough value in that.
It mght even make things better, or start to change something
that needs to change, if we both rest, and pay attention to
one another.
Yet when pressed on his statement, asked later if his ideal
audience of Ross meant that he didn't care about the public,
Gonzalez-Torres clarified:
"You know, I've said that sometimes as a joke, sometimes
seriously...."

So yes, of course, both:
a thing conceived to be so confidential and amatory that only one person can be in mind,
and then given again and again to someone else.
Because there are no limits to how mcuh we can give each other, when we recognize that none of this was ever ours to give, and as we give each other the world.

Gold Field initiated a collaborative friendship between Gonzalez-Torres and Horn.
First came a private gift, a square of gold foil sent from her to him, after the two met in 1993.
Then, gifts that were shared with everyone—
by Gonzalez-Torres, a spread of gold-foiled candy and a curtain of golden beads.
Horn returned to *Gold Field* later, but this time making two sheets.
As Gonzalez-Torres described it,
"Two, a number of companionship, of doubled pleasure, a pair, a couple, one on top of the other.
Mirroring and emanating light.
When Roni showed me this new work she said 'there is sweat in-between.'"
The gold candy, made shortly after their meeting, he called *"Untilted" (Placebo—Landscape for Roni)*.
It was an endless supply, the size and shape of which would vary from gallery to gallery, depending on the space being filled.
The candy works had what Gonzalez-Torres called an "ideal weight."
Among them, this gold candy was the heaviest, at twelve hundred pounds—
a similar piece from 1991, also called "Placebo," but with silver wrappers, comes in a close second,

while the other candy piles are at most a fraction of that
weight, typically either the weight of Ross, or of the two of
them together.
It is quite big, after all, the way that a placebo does not work—
but also, by virtue of hope, or perhaps imagination, sometimes
does.
Roni Horn began to visit Iceland regularly years before this,
in 1975.
"Having gone there, there evolved a relationship that I couldn't
separate myself from,"
she explained.
"Any place you're going to stand in, in any given moment,
is a complement to the rest of the world, historically and
empirically."
As I discuss the trip north with Simon, to Horn's Iceland and
the Thule of Greenland, I decide to keep these fantasies to
myself.
Instead, I show him how thin the gold is,
which is nice,
he says.

TRISH SALAH

Manifest

i.

Exist it, if you can. Beings that so luminesce
us alive alive—being so

Where do they go? We aspire and abandon
eat our selves and shit and sleep and eat

We drag our loves, we burn out raw, we passive
aggress our families that fail us, turn us out

We don't know where to go we shelter online
and in shelters are refused shelter often

ii.

Look up, eyes fallen asleep again,
welcome to this echo

against the redaction of being
we've grown used to

These are cuts, measure them:
acceptable, or

Tracts and declarations, pride
is a hollow you might fit in
hide, deeply

iii.

What is hidden guides more than our voices
leads through the past, to what?

What is hidden guides more than eyesight
to stutter, stumble at a human form

Guides more than touch or hearing
more than sensible becoming, acute fixture

Being only a spare measure
only rumour and glimpse

What is apparent is the ease of our death
To whom do we die? To whom wish to live?

What's to come

either past as buried or relentlessly of the present
neither recourse to urgency nor the denial of urgency

more than breaking the frame of sex's reach
more, or before, and under, what grounds?

more than the frame of the oppositional
tender proliferation, gender euphoria

beyond being counted
where they ceased to exist

breaking the frame of the oppositional
what frame is that, exactly?

2.

bios and necros and bios and necros and
as in an analytic "no"

what are the dialectics of oversight?
familiar genres of ruse or rouse,
but to re-entangle
as in human with murdered and murderable

what new humanity without purge and burn
what from the discarded and or loudly ignored
what from the rendered inoperable, non-possible
what newly new do we now passionately live?

3

either past as buried or relentlessly of the present
did somebody say literature?

Love poem

Is this spite, in repetition, in the signal back?
Is this a longed for annihilation— longed for?

What part of envy is false consciousness, or
a symptom of internalized oppression?

Too easy to envision violence
we do ourselves on that model

The horizon's market share, capitulation
as of a radical recycling already new

Leavening hunger, for visibility, for a healthy
narcissism. Why not?

Call it a solidarity of trans girls, a trauma
of trans girls? A grave of trans girls?

Is it respite from the relentless consumption
of consumption as a topic of critique of us?

Is there a dare, a bid for love, a survival equation
lust for life unburdened of fear's repetition?

Is it
what dusty winds kiss
dusk's hoped for chill, mercy of
a novice affection?

TY LITTLE

cows in suits

the government shut down
means no more manatees
to swim with
parks employees sit at home
swimming in living rooms
googling manatee videos
drowning in paper turned beer
turned choking lack of paper
cancel plans to dive
cancel family time, first
children's experience
differ from first lady's
in weight of paper
hostile political environment
too young to engage
with loved ones
on the streets, shout
"I want milk!"
you deserve it little one
to suck dry GMO
cow tits and spit it
in the face of tyrannical
leaders, you are
just learning to swim

I hate The Beatles

coo coo ca chooooooooooooo
o
o
o
o
a walrus
leaps to its death.

an escape plan
of unplanned parenthood
outside of teaching
young jump
towards what is incorporeal
fleeing towards past generations
and future science books

we are all collectively the sharp toothed
glutton, wallowing
on the precipice of
an end, unforeseen
doing our best
free climbing family
futures unfolding
amassing at the base of craggy depths

how many bodies
do we have to step
over until
we get what we want?

VALENTINE CONATY

Manifestation before love

Last night's lube blooming from
my flared pores Strips memory into ribbons
of movement and intention Becomes
desire's record related
produced Fetid lines of dried

vitality threading

across my torso Canon of repeating
fragments Narrative
with interruption and swatching
How light appears to cone from within
and imbue

that smooth surface which

touches it Soft unlit under curtain of shoulder
Whether gesture or a carefully chosen
phrase a fragment signifies
the whole of love *Do you want to come inside*
Do you want in me Who are we

to preserve our selves

in sympathetic motion Who are we
to invoke memory Ask me
toy between your lips Ask me in the penitent
whites of your wanting eyes
Who came to whom

in ribbon-weight gestural flight

Conjunctivitis

My eye already
at midnight
discharge's chartreuse
baptism My eye saturated
ducts infirm and swollen
with feminine

***

Chinatown ripe
with treacle-
sweat of ruptured trash
bags plastic run-off
The morning iridescent
with filth
en route to Apicha
for a prescribed leisure
I want to scratch itch
I want to
comb through
mascara of matted lash
To distract itch
I meet
every passing

eye Gaze
a privilege of masculine
ocularcentrism I have
usurped My plushed arcs
of flesh curtaining white
marbled pink

On Canal Street
I greet them
men and women et al.
and only men
return eye contact
I greet them
how an itch invites touch
soft and tight
lashed with contagion
Conjunctivitis' gauzy itch
excuses one from labor
an invitation
to frivol and flirt I extend
Across pearlescent
glaze of lens
crust frosts lash with white
blood cells' blunt glitter
left after sleep
tempting
to be swept away

I imagine myself
une flaneuse
kissing strangers
with my eyelashes
painting
our cheeks PINK

with contact
a transmission
liberation
from the fiction of
righteous labor
until PINK with leisure or
like an estrogenized
cock's fragile bud
flush with blood enhanced
for performative PINK
like a tongue
licking an eyeball

***

Gray eyes
spoked blue against
a pink contrast
Communing manufactured
tears I take
in a public restroom mirror
a pink-tinted selfie

A liturgical
hygiene
sponges from within
the image Mine
oversaturated 'til streaking
Cheekbones
arresting in wet light

XANDRIA PHILLIPS

NATIVITY

in the dream where I run without breasts I am motivated by flight, I haven't yet begun to unweld the framework, invent new trauma, whip the stitch arching each bosom as victuals dangled, withheld. when I hemorrhage against design it ain't incognito. the neighbors walk their dogs past me. that's me smoking in the alley, letting roses from my wrists. petal to puddle, a misgendering of matter. these hooves unhinge themselves as tiny meteors to cudgel dusk. I redress the splintering woodwork notched to my likeness, venial beneath the pomme and lilac cornucopic delight. to partake in a gender, to fashion one's self a living process of it, casting a net of postures, adornment objects, and grooming techniques into a future tense. where have I gone, and who have I built to take my place? unsuccessful at the tossing of it, I throw rocks ahead of me and predict where they will land. by virtue of touch, I am every man I manufacture my difference from. the man slipping in the mirror's moonshine enters and leaves me between my double-take, and glare into my reflection for its unregistered recognition. every night the countryside plays against my eyelids. a recurring taunt against my current location, the finale, currents of corn lapping the sun against my arms pumping with youth. the site of my making.

SOMETIMES BOYHOOD

hovering their mouths
like two men
moments before
they turn on each other

that is how the grass smells
need between boys
I wanted a love like
a shared look

so relieved to be touching
so angry it took so long
too easy to rehearse into fragility
as a boy I couldn't hide

a single soft thing
round with lemon skin
under her shirt
silken folds of fat

the boy thinks
she is a canal for shame
where goodness ends
the scent of new blood

a red scout of longing
through her private dimension
the boy tables girlhood
and the sweat is good sweat

a flock of braying gestures
shaving september grains
a cunning hunt
for each other's touch

two men sparring
over who could end
the other's suffering first
bliss shame from the body

was I not one of them
disarming a denim ilk
praying his sword would land
amidst my vast acreage

XTIAN W AND ANAÏS DUPLAN

i am not prepared is it essential to change

& i think that the mark
of a good relationship may be that it doesn't change my life
very much
at all
or
change me
i really like how non-goal oriented that is i mean srsly
should that
of course every relationship is transformative
be the
stated point?
coming out later in life like in order to
become one thing i've become

is kinda closed
cuz like risk
what if i am undone by it
i am who i am i've always been
this bae
i mean pleasure is a reason
a conversation as are all these
emotional intimacies. i keep thinking
kinds of emotional
intimacies
about this phrase "amorous friendship"
friendship WHAT
A QUEER
CONCEPT
as the thing i want most
if i have a goal for any of my
relationships

it's that they are alive
pulsing dynamic vital subject
to disruption fluctuations all that

it's so romantic!

omgx yes
friendship is SO romantic!!!

HEART EMOJI   i didn't call my dad for father's day   friendship needs
liberation

(Anaïs loved a comment)

something clicked & i--

the reason i have trouble valuing myself
is the people who raised me
didn't value me i went along
with their appraisal to preserve
our relationship i think even then
i had a sense that my own self-
worth & what people were reporting back
didn't line up i guess i figured
i must be wrong with my self-worth intact
or at least on the mend i have
no picture for what relationship is

----

currently in an uber
there in ~20min
(xtian loved a comment)

SELFIE – Anaïs + xtian
SELFIE – Anaïs + xtian
SELFIE – Anaïs + xtian
SELFIE – Anaïs + xtian
SELFIE – Anaïs + xtian
SELFIE – Anaïs + xtian
SELFIE – Anaïs + xtian
have
SELFIE – Anaïs + xtian
poems
SELFIE—Anaïs
SELFIE—Anaïs
SELFIE—Anaïs

from devin:
"Also!!! Do you happen to

PDFs or links to xtian's

from tonight? Three beers in
& we're still talking about them."

whaaaaaa !!!! my heart!

medusa's

pubes

alchemizing
childhood trauma is a dailiness
is that what adult life is lol?
(Anaïs loved a comment)
but i wanna comment on
something you said in our talkback
last night about your
poems being smarter than you

when i was living in southern appalachia
i self published like 3 or 4 chapbooks
whose content ugh like i don't even
wanna know those
poems were full of bodies
bodies changing genders
turning inside out feeling
too much or not enough
struggling i think for some
sort of articulation bodies
fucking & being fucked desires
i was so frightened of
for all i knew of trans
& queer anything then it felt like the end
of any kind of livable life
courting those possibilities--

in poem space
what i'm saying is it was all there

b4 i knew it in one sense

i was reckoning w it all in another

ZAVÉ GAYATRI MARTOHARDJONO

smoke

i saw the whole universe
in the black round of cherríe's
open mouth

she was pushing smoke
over me, ceremony

healing
is found with

being without, we pick at the
fragments of our forgotten—worse—
obliterated stories

we get lost
reach out, reach reach reach
and assume nothing is found

we spear one another
accusations blooming
bomb smoke

in the wet dark of her jaw
i saw myself

as i have been so unable to

shit, what the hell
have I built

a towering pedestal
on top of which to sit
to deny myself
blame my beloveds
for my feeling invisible
hungry, alone

the altar
in a high corner
of the dyke bar
in Doctores
    fire burns, flowers cool in water
    scarf swings, still
    a bruise blushes her eye
    slow wind

the rose bush
blooms crooked,
singed, wilted petals
behind NYPD 88th Precinct's
iron railing
    what tending
    do cops plan
    between undercover joy
    rides, SWAT raids
    interrogations
    to nourish
    budding tendrils

muscle boys grapple
atop Burger King logo

blood smears, sweat slides
them into one another
scores blink across screen

a tree tears through
concrete
roots unstoppable
gentrification realtors divesting
from their spread

smoke billows
from bowls in their hands
Indios costume-feathers flap
    black red eagle death mask
    they slap smiling gringos
    with dried greens
in the shadow of
towering pockmarked cathedral stone
engraved
by the hands of slaves
conquistador fantasias
we call history

la realidad
sometimes only
audible
in the glint of
disco-ball whirling

or hips planted
in earth

    tremors shake my bones
    call in the knowing

CONTRIBUTORS

AARON EL SABROUT is a transgender alien living on Tewa territory. He lives with his partner, his dog, and an ever-proliferating collection of succulents and spider plants. His poetry chapbook *Migration Routes* and forthcoming zine of weird trans fiction are available through his instagram @toreachpoise.

AEON GINSBERG (they/them) is a writer and performer from Baltimore City, MD. *Greyhound* (2020), their first full-length collection, was the winner of the Noemi Press 2019 Poetry Prize. In addition to writing Aeon is a Taurus, a bartender, and a bitch.

AKASHA-MITRA is a Buddhist, trans genderqueer person. They like to engage with questions of togetherness and liberation through queerness in their poetry. You can send them cat pictures at findbishaldey@gmail.com.

AMY MARVIN is a philosopher writing on humor, curiosity, care, and institutional betrayal. You can find her at @amyrmarv on Twitter.

ANAÏS DUPLAN is a trans* poet, curator, and artist. He is the author of a book of essays, *Blackspace: On the Poetics of an Afrofuture* (Black Ocean, 2020), a full-length poetry collection, *Take This Stallion* (Brooklyn Arts Press, 2016), and a chapbook, *Mount Carmel and the Blood of Parnassus* (Monster House Press, 2017). In 2016, he founded the Center for Afrofuturist Studies, an artist residency program for artists of color, based at Iowa City's artist-run organization Public Space One.

ANDREA ABI-KARAM is an arab-american genderqueer punk poet-performer cyborg, writing on the art of killing bros, the intricacies of cyborg bodies, trauma and delayed healing. Selected by Bhanu Khapil, Andrea's debut is *EXTRATRANSMISSION* (Kelsey Street Press, 2019), a poetic critique of the U.S. military's role in the War on Terror. Their second assemblage, *Villainy*, won the Les Figues Poetry Contest, selected by Simone White, and is forthcoming from Nightboat Books in Fall 2021. They are a Leo currently obsessed with queer terror and convertibles.

ARI BANIAS is the author of the book *Anybody* (W.W. Norton, 2016), and the chapbook *A Symmetry* (The Song Cave, 2018). Ari lives and teaches in the Bay Area.

BAHAAR AHSAN is a poet based in Berkeley, California. She was born and raised in San Jose, with familial roots in the Southern Iranian port city of Abadan. Like any other tgirl, Bahaar's work is both speculative and deeply embedded in lineage(s). Her writing appears in *baest*, *Amerarcana*, *Apogee*, and elsewhere.

BIANCA RAE MESSINGER is a poet and translator living in Iowa City, IA. She is the author of the digital chapbook *The Love of God* (Inpatient, 2016) and *The Land Was V There* (89+/LUMA, 2014). Her translation of Juana Isola's chapbook *You Need a Long Table...* was published by Monster House Press in 2018. *In the Jungle There Is Much to Do*, her translation of a children's book by Uruguayan anarchist Mauricio Gatti, was published by the Berlin Bienniale for Contemporary Art in 2019. She currently teaches creative writing at the University of Iowa.

BRYN KELLY was a Brooklyn-based artist of Appalachian extraction and a gossip-hoarding hairdresser. She was an active community member who contributed her talents to organizations such as SAGE, Sylvia Rivera Law Project, Camp Trans, and PERSIST. Bryn's serialized writing could be found on Showtime Network's *OurChart.com*, in digital literary magazine *PrettyQueer.com*, and pseudonymously as Dearhussy and Partybottom on Tumblr. Bryn's work was printed in the collections *Trans/Love: Radical Sex,*

Love and Relationships Beyond the Gender Binary, *Trans Women Across Genres*, and *Time is Not A Line: Reflections on HIV/AIDS Now*, commissioned by the New Museum. In 2013, she was selected as a Lambda Literary Fellow. She cofounded Theater Transgression, a transgender multimedia performance collective, co-created the touring roadshow *The Fully Functional Cabaret*, and performed for Visual AIDS, the Whitney Museum, *TRIPS*, *Low Standards*, *SQUIRTS*, and *Queer Memoir*.

CACONRAD received a 2019 Creative Capital grant and has also received a Pew Fellowship in the Arts, as well as *The Believer* Magazine Book Award and The Gil Ott Book Award. The author of 9 books of poetry and essays, *While Standing in Line for Death* (Wave Books) won the 2018 Lambda Book Award. They teach at Columbia University in New York City, and Sandberg Art Institute in Amsterdam. Please look for CA's books and the documentary *The Book of Conrad* from Delinquent Films online at http://bit.ly/88CAConrad.

CAELAN ERNEST is a poet performer living in Brooklyn, NY. Their work considers seriality as a model to explore how digital topias allow the queer body to undergo multiple puberties. They hold an MFA in Writing from Pratt Institute & are publicist at Nightboat Books. Hit them (& their cat named Salad) up on social media: @transputation.

CALLIE GARDNER is a poet and editor from Glasgow, Scotland. Their book-length poem *naturally it is not.* is published by the87press, and their critical book *Poetry & Barthes* by Liverpool University Press. They edit the magazine *Zarf Poetry* and its associated pamphlet press, Zarf Editions. Other work circulates at calyxpo.wordpress.com & @calyxpo.

CAMERON AWKWARD-RICH is an assistant professor of Women, Gender, Sexuality Studies at the University of Massachusetts Amherst. He is the author of two poetry collections – *Sympathetic Little Monster* (Ricochet Editions, 2016) and *Dispatch* (Persea Books, 2019). His other writing can be found in *Signs*, *Science Fiction Studies*, *American Quarterly*, *Transgender Studies Quarterly*, and elsewhere.

CASPAR HEINEMANN is an itinerant nondenominational gay poet and artist from London, UK, interested in counterculture, mysticism, springtime, and irreverence. His first poetry collection *Novelty Theory* was published in 2019 by the87press.

CHARLES THEONIA is a poet and teacher from Brooklyn, where they're working to externalize interior femme landscapes. They are the author of art book *Saw Palmettos*, on hormones, community, and the brain-time continuum (Container, 2018) and the chapbook *Which One Is the Bridge* (Topside Press, 2015).

CHING-IN CHEN is a genderqueer Chinese American hybrid writer, community organizer and teacher. They are author of *The Heart's Traffic* (Arktoi/Red Hen Press, 2009) and recombinant (Kelsey Street Press, 2017; winner of the 2018 Lambda Literary Award for Transgender Poetry) as well as the chapbooks *how to make black paper sing* (speCt! Books, 2019) and Kundiman for Kin :: Information Retrieval for Monsters (forthcoming from Portable Press at Yo-Yo Labs and a Finalist for the Leslie Scalapino Award). Chen is also the co-editor of *The Revolution Starts at Home: Confronting Intimate Violence Within Activist Communities* (South End Press, 2011; AK Press 2016) and *Here Is a Pen: an Anthology of West Coast Kundiman Poets* (Achiote Press, 2009). They have received fellowships from Kundiman, Lambda, Watering Hole, Can Serrat and Imagining America and are a part of Macondo and Voices of Our Nations Arts Foundation writing communities. A community organizer, they have worked in Asian American communities in San Francisco, Oakland, Riverside, Boston, Milwaukee and Houston. They are currently an Assistant Professor in the School of Interdisciplinary Arts and Sciences and the MFA in Creative Writing and Poetics at the University of Washington Bothell.

CLARA ZORNADO is a trans musician, writer, and performer who lives in Providence, Rhode Island. They write many letters, but publicize them infrequently. Clara is currently letting go of firmer discretion to make room for an open-hearted embrace of the epistolary.

CODY-ROSE CLEVIDENCE is the Author of *BEAST FEAST* and *Flung/Throne*, both from Ahsahta, and several chapbooks. They live in the Arkansas Ozarks with their medium-sized but lion-hearted dog, Birdie.

CYRÉE JARELLE JOHNSON is a writer and librarian from Piscataway, New Jersey. *SLINGSHOT*, his first book of poetry, was published by Nightboat Books in 2019. Find Cyrée online at cyreejarellejohnson.com or @cyreejarelle.

EVAN KLEEKAMP was a 2019 Creative Capital | The Andy Warhol Foundation Arts Writers Grant Finalist. Their writing has appeared in *X-TRA*, *Open Space* (SFMOMA), and the *Los Angeles Review of Books*. Apogee Graphics will release a limited-edition excerpt of their novel, *Double Negative II*, in 2020. Their research interests include: disability, prosthesis, psychoanalysis, and the lecture-performance.

FAYE CHEVALIER is a Philadelphia-based poet and essayist. She is the author of the chapbooks *future.txt* (Empty Set Press 2018) and *flesh_wound* (Accidental Player 2020), and her work has been featured in *The Wanderer*, *Peach Mag*, *Witch Craft Magazine*, *the tiny*, and elsewhere. Some of her awards and recognitions include being the first poet ever to have work published in a cyberpunk tabletop RPG podcast (Neoscum 2018) and also a Pushcart nomination. Find her on Twitter where she cries about cyborgs, vampires, and having a body at @bratcore.

HARRY JOSEPHINE GILES is from Orkney and lives in Leith. Their latest book is *The Games* from Out-Spoken Press, shortlisted for the 2016 Edwin Morgan Poetry Award. They have a PhD in Creative Writing from Stirling, co-direct the performance platform Anatomy, are now touring the poetry-music-video show *Drone*. www.harryjosephine.com.

HAZEL AVERY is a poet currently based in philadelphia. her work is readily available online. she urges you to consider providing direct material aid to homeless folks.

HOLLY RAYMOND is a PhD candidate at Temple University, where she teaches creative writing. Her chapbook *Mall is Lost* was published by Adjunct Press in 2018 and *Heaven's Wish to Destroy All Minds* is forthcoming from Marlskarx. Other work has appeared in *Bedfellows*, *Paintbucket*, *The Volta*, *boneless skinless*, and elsewhere.

IAN KHARA ELLASANTE is a Black, queer, trans-nonbinary poet and cultural studies scholar. Winner of the 49th New Millennium Award for Poetry, Ian Khara's poems have appeared in The Feminist Wire, The Volta: Evening Will Come, Hinchas de Poesía, cur.ren.cy, and elsewhere. With abiding affection for their hometown of Memphis, Ian Khara has also loved living and writing in Tucson, Brooklyn, and most recently, in southern Maine, where they are an assistant professor of gender and sexuality studies at Bates College. Jackie Ess is a poet and novelist. No plugs or pedigrees for the moment, but keep your eye out.

JAMIE TOWNSEND is a genderqueer poet and editor living in Oakland. They are half-responsible for *Elderly*, an ongoing publishing experiment and hub of ebullience and disgust. They are the author of *Pyramid Song* (above/ground press, 2018), and *Sex Machines* (blush, 2019) and *Shade* (Elis Press, 2015). An essay on the literary magazine *Soup* was published in *The Bigness of Things: New Narrative and Visual Culture* (Wolfman Books, 2017). They are the editor of *Beautiful Aliens: A Steve Abbott Reader* (Nightboat, 2019) and *Libertines in the Ante-Room of Love: Poets on Punk* (Jet Tone, 2019).

JAYSON KEERY lives in Western Mass, where they attend the MFA for Poets and Writers at the University of Massachusetts Amherst. They are the assistant managing editor of *jubilat* and the poetry editor for *Cosmonauts Avenue*. They host the Majestic Queer Lit Club reading series and the HUT reading series in Northampton, MA. You can follow their reading series and publications on Instagram @mostly_like_being_left_alone and on Twitter @JaysonKeery.

JESI GASTON is a writer and filmmaker based in Chicago. They're also the poetry & prose editor for *Homintern Magazine*. They're currently working on a full-length manuscript about the Marx Brothers, from which these pieces are excerpted. Previously, another excerpt from this project, "MY POEM ABOUT GROUCHO MARX," was published on *Queen Mob's Teahouse*.

JESSICA BET is a trans toad, or white wom-n. Her two chapbooks are *Call It Pleasure* (2017) and *Because I Must...(*2018). Her work has appeared on the internet; in various Instagram posts; in *The Brooklyn Rail*; and the Topos Press collection *It Was Over When You Said What* (2016). More is available at anothernightanotherdream.com. Bet was born—and resides currently—in the state of Maryland.

JIMMY COOPER is a minnesota poet, fake punk, and zinester. they have been described as "bad and loud," a "heartthrob," and "interesting," whatever that means. their debut chapbook, *honey, i think it's time we started seeing other vandals* came out in september 2019, and you can find them on twitter @ immmortellle or instagram @anarchimmortelle.

JO BARCHI is a writer/editor/ice cream scooper/faggot living in Chicago. Their work can be found in *Joyland Mag*, *Triangle House Review*, *Hobart*, and *Peach Mag*.

JOSÉ DÍAZ is a queer Latinx poet and writer from San Jose, California. They studied creative writing at the University of California, Santa Cruz and currently work as a bookseller in Cambridge, MA. When not letting their fruit spoil, José is teaching themself InDesign to make poetry chapbooks.

JOSHUA JENNIFER ESPINOZA is a trans woman poet living in California. Her work has been featured in *Poetry*, *Denver Quarterly*, *American Poetry Review*, *Buzzfeed*, *Poem-a-Day*, *Lambda Literary*, *The Offing*, and elsewhere. She is the author of *THERE SHOULD BE FLOWERS* (Civil Coping Mechanisms 2016) and *I'm Alive. It Hurts. I Love It.* (2014; reprinted via Big Lucks 2019).

JOSS BARTON is a writer, journalist, and spoken word performance artist exploring and documenting queer and trans* life, love, and liberation. Her work blends femme-fever dreams over the soundtrack of the American nightmare. She resides and writes in Saint Louis, Missouri.

JULIAN TALAMANTEZ BROLASKI is the author of *Of Mongrelitude* (Wave Books 2017, a finalist for the Lambda Literary Award for Transgender Poetry), *Advice for Lovers* (City Lights 2012), *gowanus atropolis* (Ugly Duckling Presse 2011), and numerous chapbooks. It is the lead singer and rhythm guitarist of Juan & the Pines, and formerly of The Western Skyline. Julian maintains a blog of handwritten poems at https://julianspoems.tumblr.com/.

KAMDEN HILLIARD prefers KAM. They are child and sibling of the Hilliard family, graduate of Punahou School, Sarah Lawrence College, The University of Hawai'i at Mānoa, and the Iowa Writers' Workshop. They have published three chapbooks of poetry: *Distress Tolerance* (Magic Helicopter Press, 2016), *Perceived Distance from Impac*t (2017, Black Lawrence Press) and, *henceforce: a travel poetic* (Omnidawn Books, 2019). While you can find Kam's writing in lovely places like *The Black Warrior Review*, *West Branch*, *Bennington Review*, *Best Experimental American Poetry*, and *Prairie Schooner*, these days they are serving an Americorps VISTA year in Greenville, SC. Find Kam on the internet at kamdenihilliard.com. Bring them to your venue. Say hello.

KASHIF SHARMA-PATEL is a writer, poet and editor at the87press. They work at the interface of sonic, visual and written cultures with particular reference to queer and racialised experimental work. Kashif has published and performed poetry across a number of platforms with a full-length collection forthcoming. They also write music, art and literary criticism for *Artforum*, *The Quietus*, *AQNB*, *Poetry London* and more.

KAY GABRIEL is a poet and essayist. She's the author of *Kissing Other People or the House of Fame* (Rosa Press, 2021). Kay has received fellowships from the Poetry Project, Lambda Literary and Princeton University, where she recently completed her PhD. She's a member of the editorial collective of the Poetry Project Newsletter.

LAUREL UZIELL is a writer, communist, and various strawmen from the north of England, currently based in London. She writes for and with friends, comrades, lovers, and especially enemies, and as such all their work is collectively written. Publications include *Instant Cop Death* (Shit Valley, 2017) and *T* (Materials, forthcoming).

LESLIE FEINBERG, who identified as an anti-racist white, working-class, secular Jewish, transgender, lesbian, female, revolutionary communist, died on November 15, 2014. She/zie succumbed to complications from multiple tick-borne co-infections, including Lyme disease, babeisiosis, and protomyxzoa rheumatica, after decades of illness. Zie/she died at home in Syracuse, NY, with hir partner and spouse of 22 years, Minnie Bruce Pratt, at hir side. Hir last words were: *"Remember me as a revolutionary communist."*

LEVI BENTLEY is a 2019 LAMBDA Literary Fellow, Director of Pedagogy for Blue Stoop, and 2017 Leeway Art and Change grantee. They live in Philadelphia where they make chapbooks with Ted Rees under the imprint Asterion Projects. Poems from "Bucolic Eclogue" were released by Lamehouse Press in 2016. They have also released chapbooks through 89plus/LUMA Foundation, Damask Press, and Well Greased Press. Poems have appeared in *Apiary*, *Bedfellows*, *BlazeVOX*, *Elective Affinities*, *Fact-Simile*, *Painted Bride Quarterly*, *The Rupture*, *Stillwater Review*, *The Wanderer*, and a variety of other venues.

LIAM OCTOBER O'BRIEN grew up on a small island. His poetry and prose can be found in the HIV Here & Now Project, *New South*, *The Iowa Review*, the Lambda Literary Spotlight, *Electric Literature*, *A&U Magazine*, and the *Denver Quarterly*. He completed his MFA at the Iowa Writers' Workshop, where he was an Iowa Arts Fellow. He is one of the founding editors of *Vetch: A Magazine of Trans Poetry & Poetics*.

LISTEN CHEN is an editor of *The Volcano* newspaper and a member of Red Braid Alliance, an anti-colonial and anti-capitalist organization fighting for social revolution. They live on occupied Coast Salish Territories in Vancouver, Canada.

LOGAN FEBRUARY is a non-binary Nigerian poet and graduate student at Purdue University's MFA program in Creative Writing. They and their work have been featured in The Guardian Life, Dazed, The Rumpus, Lambda Literary, Washington Square Review, Africa In Dialogue, and more. They are the author of *In The Nude* (PANK Books, 2021) and three chapbooks.

LOU SULLIVAN (b. 1951, Milwaukee; d. 1991, San Francisco) was a writer, activist, typesetter, trans historian, and queer revolutionary. Sullivan wrote for the *Advocate*, *GPU News*, and *Metamorphosis*. He also prepared newsletters for the trans organizations Golden Gate Girls/Guys and FTM. Organized by Sullivan, FTM was the first peer-support group for trans men. Sullivan also published "Information for the Female-to-Male Crossdresser and Transsexual", a practical guidebook, and *From Female to Male: The Life of Jack Bee Garland*, a biography. Sullivan left 8.4 cubic feet of archival material from his life and studies to the GLBT Historical Society, of which he was a founding member. The content of the archive includes his extensive diaries as well as photographs, short stories, poems, essays, video tapes, correspondences, medical research files and important primary sources related to transgender history.

MAI SCHWARTZ is a poet and translator whose work has been supported by fellowships from the Leeway Foundation, the Yiddish Book Center, and the Bread Loaf Writers Conference. Raised in New Jersey and refined in Philadelphia, he currently lives in New York. His dream as a poet is to write a libretto.

MAXE CRANDALL is a poet and playwright whose work engages experimental forms in political contexts. His book about AIDS archives and generational memory, *The Nancy Reagan Collection*, is forthcoming from Futurepoem. Maxe produces a Poets Theater series at The Stud in San Francisco.

MILES A.M. COLLINS-SIBLEY received their MFA in Poetry from UMass-Amherst's program for Poets & Writers and is currently a PhD student in UMass-Amherst's African American Studies department. They're an alum of Winter Tangerine's Catalyzing Self Revolutions workshop and their poems can be found in *McSweeney's Internet Tendency*, *The Felt*, *Peach Mag*, *poets.org*, Split

Lip Press' 2019 Anthology, *TRACK//FOUR*, *Black Warrior Review*, and *Crab Fat Magazine*. You can follow them on Twitter and Instagram @miles_n__miles.

NAT RAHA is a poet, activist and scholar living in Edinburgh, Scotland. Her poetry includes *of sirens, body & faultlines* (Boiler House Press, 2018), *countersonnets* (Contraband Books, 2013), and *Octet* (Veer Books, 2010). Her poetry is of an innovative, condensed and politicised lyric, speaking of marginal forms of living and queer desires, feeling through feminist diasporas and generative constraints. Her work has been translated into French, German, Greek, Portuguese and Spanish. Nat holds a PhD in Creative & Critical Writing from the University of Sussex, UK, and co-edits the zine *Radical Transfeminism*.

NATALIE MESNARD is a writer and game designer based in NYC, where they teach Narrative Design at Pratt Institute and direct E-Line Media's game design learning programs. They did their MFA in Fiction and taught Creative Writing at the University of Illinois at Urbana-Champaign, and have published poetry, fiction, and nonfiction in *Blackbird*, *The Kenyon Review*, *The Gettysburg Review*, *Ninth Letter*, and elsewhere. Natalie has done digital marketing at Grove Atlantic, championed small press publishing as Communications Director at CLMP, and read submissions for A Public Space and One Story. They have also taught at the Hudson Valley Writers Center, and with the Kenyon Review Young Writers Workshop.

NEON MASHUROV (NM Esc) is a poet, music writer and culture worker from Brooklyn and the post-Soviet diaspora, writing on collectivity; utopias & dystopias; and queer & trans legacies of care in relation to the ambient violence of the surveillance state. Their poetry has appeared in *The Felt*, *Peach Mag*, *Ghost City Press*, and many a punk-printed chapzine.

NICOLAS "NICO" DAVID GOGAN (1/1/92-11/1/19) was born on New Year's Day to parents, Michael and Linda Riehl. He is also survived by one younger, biological sister, Lilith; however he was considered family by many more. He graduated with a Bachelor's degree from Kansas City Art Institute, having majored in Illustration. Despite that focus, he was a multidisciplinary artist and also produced a prolific amount of work in other media. In his personal life, Nico was also a loud and proud member of the Queer and Trans communities, having identified as a transsexual male himself. Both his work and identity culminated in his final work as a tattoo artist. Though he only worked for around a year before his untimely death, Nico was able to leave a proud legacy of work emblazoned upon the skin of countless young queer and trans people.

NOAH LEBIEN is a poet and performer living in Brooklyn. Graduated from Shimer College and received their MFA from Bennington College. Published in *GenderFail*, *Prelude*, *Crab Fat Magazine*, among others. Currently developing music/performance pieces using Max/MSP/Jitter and motion sensor technology to experiment with the expanse of the queer body in resonant space. Poetry chapbook coming out from Wendy's Subway. Music at https://noahlebien.bandcamp.com/.

NORA FULTON is a poet and academic living in Montreal. She is the author of three collections of poetry: *Life Experience Coolant* (Bookthug 2013), *Presence Detection System* (Hiding Press 2019), and *Thee Display* (Anteism/ Documents 2020). Her writing and critical work has appeared in *Social Text*, *Music and Literature*, *Ossa Magazine*, *Radical Philosophy* and elsewhere.

NORA TREATBABY is a queer writer in transit between all things. She does not spend her time.

PEACH KANDER is a queer poet and current MFA candidate in poetry at NYU. They are the poetry editor of *Washington Square Review*, and sometimes go to karaoke to sing classic pop songs in the style of Bob Dylan. Poems can be found in *Peach Mag*, *Landfill Journal*, *Fugue*, and *dirt child, vol. 1*, and other creative property can be found in the Sephora archives.

RACHEL FRANKLIN WOOD is a trans poet from Laramie, Wyoming, though she hasn't actually lived there for a while. She currently resides in Colorado, where she is a co-editor of *pulpmouth* and MFA candidate at the University of

Colorado - Boulder. Her chapbook, *Every Spring Underneath*, is available from Dancing Girl Press.

RAQUEL SALAS RIVERA (Mayagüez, 1985) is a Puerto Rican poet, translator, and literary critic. In 2018, they were named the Poet Laureate of Philadelphia for a two-year term. The following year they became the inaugural recipient of the Laureate Fellowship from the Academy of American Poets and won the New Voices Award from Puerto Rico's Festival de la Palabra. Their third book, *lo terciario/the tertiary* (2nd ed., Noemi Press, 2019), was on the 2018 National Book Award Longlist and won the 2018 Lambda Literary Award for Transgender Poetry. Their fifth book, *x/ex/exis: poemas para la nación/ poems for the nation* was the first recipient of the Ambroggio Prize (Editorial Bilingüe/ Bilingual Press, 2020). They live and work in Puerto Rico.

RAY FILAR is a writer, artist and PhD student in Creative Writing and Gender Studies at Sussex University. They are currently working on a novel about work, sex, drugs and criminalization. They often perform in drag as their alter-ego That Ray, and performances include: Tate Britain and Modern, Hayward Gallery, Institute of Contemporary Arts, Glastonbury and Latitude festivals, and Cologne Art Week. Twitter: @rayfilar / Insta: @itsthat_ray.

ROCKET CALESHU is a writer based in Los Angeles.

ROWAN POWELL is a writer, PhD candidate at UC Santa Cruz, and publisher with pssss.co. They grew up in rural South West England, and spent several years in London, before moving to the West Coast.

SAMUEL ACE is a trans/genderqueer poet and sound artist. He is the author of several books, most recently *Our Weather Our Sea* (Black Radish 2019), the newly re-issued *Meet Me There: Normal Sex* and *Home in three days. Don't wash.*, (Belladonna* Germinal Texts 2019), and *Stealth* with poet Maureen Seaton. He is the recipient of the Astraea Lesbian Writer Award and the Firecracker Alternative Book Award in Poetry, as well as a two-time finalist for both the Lambda Literary Award and the National Poetry Series. His work has been widely anthologized and recent poems can be found in *Poetry*, *PEN America*, *Best American Experimental Poetry*, *Vinyl*, and many other journals and anthologies.

STEPHEN ELIZABETH IRA is a writer and performer. His work has appeared or is forthcoming in *Fence*, *Poetry*, and other venues. He was a co-founder and co-editor of *Vetch: A Magazine of Trans Poetry and Poetics*. Ira has shown solo performance work at venues like La MaMa ETC, directed several short plays, and originated roles in new works by Maxe Crandall and Bernadette Mayer. In 2013, he was a Lambda Literary Fellow. He studied poetry at the Iowa Writers' Workshop.

SYLVIA RIVERA (1951-2002): A revolutionary of the 1969 Stonewall uprising, Sylvia was a tireless advocate for all those who have been marginalized as the "gay rights" movement has mainstreamed. Sylvia fought hard against the exclusion of transgender people from the Sexual Orientation Non-Discrimination Act in New York, established STAR (Street Transvestite Action Revolutionaries) and was a loud and persistent voice for the rights of people of color and low-income queers and trans people.

T FLEISCHMANN is the author of *Time Is the Thing a Body Moves Through* and *Syzygy, Beauty*.

Born in Halifax, TRISH SALAH is the author of the Lambda award winning *Wanting in Arabic*, and of *Lyric Sexology Vol. 1*. She was shortlisted for the Dayne Ogilvie prize for LGBTQ writers in 2018 and is currently an associate professor of Gender Studies at Queen's University.

Poet TY LITTLE is currently living in Richmond, Virginia where they are studying Religion and Literature at Virginia Commonwealth University. Their work has been published in *Wonder*, *Landfill*, and elsewhere.

VALENTINE CONATY is a Birmingham-grown artist and editor based in Queens. They founded *Bomb Cyclone*, an online journal of ecopoetics and mixed media art, in 2018. They also edit for Roof Books. They were the recipient of the VIDA Review Fellowship for Women and Non-Binary Writers at Sundress Academy for the Arts in 2019. Work may be found in *Anomaly*, The Operating System's *Ex-Spec Po* series, Glass Poetry's *Poets Resist* series, *Prelude*—and elsewhere under various former aliases.

XANDRIA PHILLIPS is a writer, educator, and visual artist from rural Ohio. The recipient of the Judith A. Markowitz Award for Emerging Writers, Xandria has received fellowships from Brown University, Callaloo, Cave Canem, The Conversation Literary Festival, Oberlin College, and the Wisconsin Institute for Creative Writing. Their poetry has been featured in *American Poetry Review, Black Warrior Review, BOMB Magazine, Crazyhorse, Poets.org, and Virginia Quarterly Review.* Xandria's poem, "For a Burial Free of Sharks" won the *GIGANTIC Sequins* Poetry Contest judged by Lucas de Lima. Xandria's chapbook, *Reasons for Smoking* is the winner of the 2016 Seattle Review Chapbook Contest judged by Claudia Rankine. Their first book, *HULL* was published by Nightboat Books in 2019 and is the winner of the 2020 Lambda Literary Award for Trans Poetry.

XTIAN W is a trans femme poet, essayist, & performance artist. Originally from the american south, they currently live, work, & paint their nails in Brooklyn, NY.

ZAVÉ GAYATRI MARTOHARDJONO is a performance-maker and dance artist. They dream of being a poet. They collaborate with artists to dig up body memory, consider anti-colonial and anti-assimilationist practices, and tell forgotten stories. zavemartohardjono.com, @zavozavito.

PRIOR PUBLICATIONS

ANDREA ABI-KARAM

"TO THE COP WHO READ MY TEXT MESSAGES" is excerpted from *EXTRATRANSMISSION* (Kelsey Street Press, 2019). "HOLD MY HAND" previously appeared in *Baest*.

BAHAAR AHSAN

"cut the apricot in half remove the pit the pit can only get in your way" previously appeared in *Berkeley Poetry Review*.

BRYN KELLY

"Diving Into the Wreck" previously appeared on Bryn Kelly's blog, brynkelly-blog.tumblr.com. Reprinted with permission of the estate.

CAMERON AWKWARD-RICH

"Everywhere We Look, There We Are" from *Dispatch*. Copyright © 2019 by Cameron Awkward-Rich. Used by permission of Persea Books, Inc (New York), www.perseabooks.com. All rights reserved.

CHARLES THEONIA

"The People's Beach" previously appeared in *Triangle House*. "The Color of Joy is Pink" will appear in *GUTS*.

CYRÉE JARELLE JOHNSON

"harold mouthfucks THE DEVIL" from *SLINGSHOT*, copyright 2019 by Cyrée Jarelle Johnson. Reprinted with the permission of the author and Nightboat Books.

FAYE CHEVALIER

"feral & not masc enough for a shoulder tattoo" previously appeared in *Occulum.*

HOLLY RAYMOND

"Secret Mission Orders for Goblin Romantic" and "One or Several Goblin Girl Workers Dreaming in Unison of the Mothman" are excerpted from *Mall is Lost* (Adjunct Press, 2018).

JOSS BARTON

A version of pink_sissy will appear in *BELT* magazine.

JULIAN TALAMANTEZ BROLASKI

"against breeding," "in the cut," "on loneliness," from *Of Mongrelitude*, copyright 2017 by Julian Talamantez Brolaski. Reprinted with the permission of the author and Wave Books.

KAY GABRIEL

"You Say Wife" previously appeared in *Social Text*. "I Could Go On" previously appeared in *The Recluse.*

LESLIE FEINBERG

"Letter to Teresa" by Leslie Feinberg is excerpted from the 20th anniversary edition of *Stone Butch Blues*, first published by Firebrand Books in 1993. Reprinted with permission of The Estate of Leslie Feinberg. Go to lesliefeinberg.net for a free PDF download of *Stone Butch Blues.*

LIAM O'BRIEN

"Companion Poetica" previously appeared in the *Lambda Literary Poetry Spotlight.*

LOU SULLIVAN

From *We Both Laughed in Pleasure: The Selected Diaries of Lou Sullivan, 1961–1991*, published by Nightboat Books. Reprinted with permission of Courtesy of Gay, Lesbian, Bisexual, Transgender Historical Society.

PEACH KANDER

"love is / a rat" previously appeared in *Peach Mag*.

ROCKET CALESHU

"Feye" previously appeared in *TAMMY*.

SYLVIA RIVERA

Sylvia Rivera (July 1951-February 2002) gave the speech "Bitch On Wheels" at NYC Pride in June 2001. The editors encountered the speech in *Street Transvestite Action Revolutionaries: Survival, Revolt, and Queer Antagonist Struggle* (Untorelli Press, 2013). An exhaustive effort has been made to locate all rights holders and to clear reprint permissions. This process has been complicated, and if any required acknowledgements have been omitted, or any rights overlooked, it is unintentional and forgiveness is requested.

T FLEISCHMANN

This excerpt is reprinted by permission from *Time Is the Thing a Body Moves Through* (Coffee House Press, 2019). Copyright © 2019 by T Flesichmann.

ACKNOWLEDGMENTS

The editors compiled *We Want It All* in occupied Lenapehoking. We acknowledge that we live on the unceded territory of the Lenni Lenape, Canarsie, Shinnecock and Munsee peoples. We acknowledge the many Indigenous Nations with ties to this land and we recognize that the Lenape still call Manahatta home. We assert solidarity with dispossessed and colonized people from Wet'suwet'en to Palestine.

Our thanks to Brian Hochberger, Caelan Ernest, Cam Scott, Elliott Sky Case, Grace Byron, Jaye Elizabeth Elijah, Lina Bergamini, Lindsey Boldt, Lix Z, Mike Funk, and Stephen Motika for their dedicated support of this project, manifest in countless hours of discussion, editing, proofing, design and care.

To our contributors: this book is yours.

To our friends, lovers, abolitionist family, fellow organizers, collaborative freaks, perverts, poets: Adelaide Penelope, Adjua Gargi Nzinga Greaves, Aldrin Valdez, Amy De'Ath, Andrea Lawlor, Andrea Marina, Andrew Brooks, Angel Dominguez, Anna Gurton-Wachter, Ara Jo, Astrid Lorange, Bayley Blaisdell, Becca Teich, Binx Yglecias, Brandon English, Bug, Caitlin Lowell, Cam Scott, Casey Plett, Cecilia Gentili, Celia Cooper, Ceyenne Doroshow, Chillian Sherard, Chris Nealon, Ciarán, Claire Grossman, Constance Augusta Zaber, Cyd Nova, Dagan Brown, Danny Thanh Nguyen, Davey Davis, Denise Benavides, Diana Hamilton, Disha Karnad Jani, Divya Victor, Dorsey Bass, Elena Comay del Junco, emji spero, Emma Heaney, Eric Kostiuk-Williams,

Erika Hodges, Etel Adnan, Evan Raczynski, Gabrielle Civil, Gaines Parker, Gia Gonzales, Graeme Lamb, Greg Nissan, Hal Schrieve, Harron Walker, Ian Dreiblatt, Imani Elizabeth Jackson, Ivanna Baranova, Jackie Ess, Jasbir Puar, Jasmine Gibson, Jay Dehner, jayy dodd, Jo Barchi, jo valdés, Joel Gregory, John Rufo, Jordy Rosenberg, Josh Billings, Joshua Clover, Juleon Robinson, Jules Gleeson, Jules Onrubia, Juliana Spahr, Juliana Delgado Lopera, Kamelya Omayma Youssef, Katia Perea, Kevin Killian, Khalil, Kneejay, Kyle Dacuyan, Lana Barkawi, Lara Durback, Leila Weefur, Lena Afridi, Lena Solow, Lenora, Liam O'Brien, Lisa F., the other Lisas, Lix Z, Liz Rose, Lou Cornum, Luke Roberts, mai c. doan, Malina Buturovic, Marie Buck, Marwa Helal, Mathura Umachandran, Max, Maya Songbird, merritt k, Michelle O'Brien, Mike Funk, Morgan M. Page, Morgan Vo, Mounia Abousaid, Muna Mire, Nailah Taman, Naomi Shihab Nye, Nicole Wallace, Nine Yamamoto, NM Esc, noah ross, Parker Menzimer, Philip Metres, Rami Karim, Raquel Namuche, Rebecca Bulnes, Riley Mang, Río Sofia, Rosa Marin, Rosario Inés, Ry Dunn, Rylee Lyman, Sahar Khraibani, Serge Rodriguez, Sergio, Shiv Kotecha, Simi, Solmaz Sharif, Sophie Jones, Sophie Lewis, Stacy Szymaszek, Suzy Exposito, Stephen Ira, Talitha Kearey, Tanya Nguyen, Thora Siemsen, Tom Davies, Tom Foxall, Tongo Eisen-Martin, Torrey Peters, Valérie Reding, Victoria X, Wendy Trevino, Will Hughes, Xavier, Yanyi, Zeyn Joukhadar. Bryn Kelly's essay in this volume quotes the late activist Frances Goldin: "Your life will be made sweet by comrades and friends," as you make ours.

NIGHTBOAT BOOKS

Nightboat Books, a nonprofit organization, seeks to develop audiences for writers whose work resists convention and transcends boundaries. We publish books rich with poignancy, intelligence, and risk. Please visit nightboat.org to learn about our titles and how you can support our future publications.

The following individuals have supported the publication of this book. We thank them for their generosity and commitment to the mission of Nightboat Books:

Kazim Ali
Anonymous
Jean C. Ballantyne
Photios Giovanis
Amanda Greenberger
Elizabeth Motika
Benjamin Taylor
Peter Waldor
Jerrie Whitfield & Richard Motika

In addition, this book has been made possible, in part, by grants from the New York City Department of Cultural Affairs in partnership with the City Council and the New York State Council on the Arts Literature Program.